I was raised by women who put moldy bread out in the yard. They would call us downstairs in the middle of the night to see what the scraps of the day attracted. They would whisper to us, *come and see... be slow and quiet* as we tiptoed down the stairs and cupped our hands around our eyes, resting tiny foreheads on the inky backdoor glass. We'd stand there, three, four, five divers in goggles made of hands, peering into the forever abyss of the woods at night.

Flipping the switch was like turning on the sun, revealing swatches of brown, pink, black, orange. Shapes fuzzed and molecules shifted as our eyes adjusted, landing on slick snouts and shiny fur, legs short and tall connecting to round feet touching grass. So often it was a fox, the same one we'd see on an occasional Sunday afternoon, grinning and sniffing heaps of wheat and corn or whatever went bad in the fridge, happy under the wrinkled covers of darkness. Sometimes she was alone, but other times she was packed in next to possums, skunks, an occasional deer, bunched together atop the grass hill that collided with our backyard's stone wall.

They were lifted to be level with our eyes, posed over old food on three sides. A family at a sitcom dinner table. For a while, there was an all-white skunk with red eyes who would come to feast at night. At first we didn't know what type of animal he was, pressed in for feeding next to the other skunks, but he was my favorite: not just a waddling ball of fur that disappeared quickly into darkness, but instead he floated across land like a beacon, a small bright cloud that even when trying to hide, was so utterly, pathetically visible.

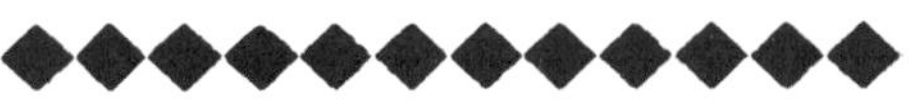

Nociception

As he exited the Coney Island-bound F train one summer evening, the turnstile, either damp from the humidity or moist from an unknown source, shifted his attention toward the earth. There, between the gait of his step and the threshold of the train was a giant silk moth. Its reddish-brown patterned wings looked like a sunset over a burning city and extended nearly the length of his shoe. Without hesitation, he bent at the waist and reached his hands out toward the moth, moving his fingers in slow deliberate increments to avoid touching the powder silken wings. He could see the moth was suffering, its red furry abdomen punctured, its insides exposed to the air. He recalled a study Harvard had published, where, after torturing fruit flies for extended periods, they had discerned insects feel acute and chronic pain. Nociception was the term they used. Now, he felt guilt whenever he slaughtered the diligent stream of ants emerging from the separating wood floors of his ground-floor apartment.

(*continued on page 19*)

CUT OUT THIS PICTURE AND DIP IT IN HONEY

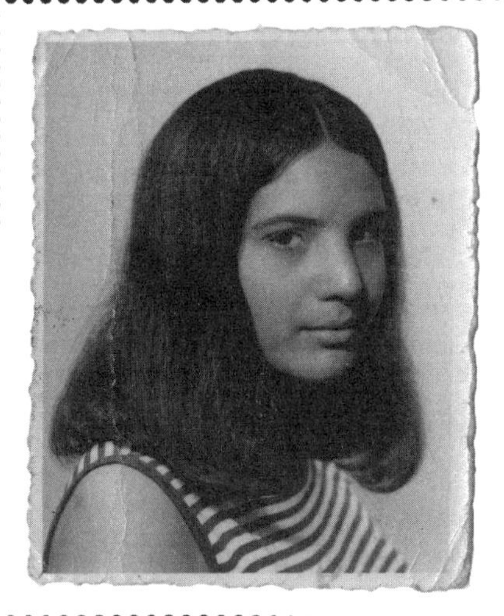

mère

c'était ton nom
c'est comme cela que je te nommais

mère, océan qui gronde et engloutit
mère, qui vomit les mots qui blessent
mère, cicatrice

jamais ne se referme

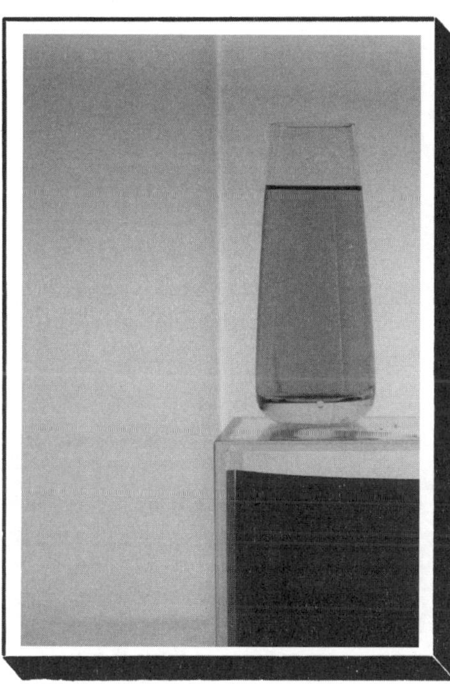

CHOREOGRAPHY FOR A RAINSTORM

When it rains in the afternoon, the rain is a spell. The window hangs from ceiling to floor. Frame outside and watch the sky cascade. Adjust your arms to match the storm's capacity for water.

When you are also so much water, what movement is fitting?

The window is a spell as it hangs from ceiling to floor. Catch the eye of your outline which lingers in the glass. Turn your desk to parallel the window and become still.

Your reflection winks out of sync. The window is a spell as you wonder where else it is raining and who also looks through a window this moment to seek cues for movement.

While it is still raining, turn your desk to face the window. Turn your face. Lean forward. In the glass, you return to yourself. The plant behind you doubles and reaches, tendrils toward you or toward the rain.

You notice the sky's new violet and startle that the afternoon will soon be over.

On the grass, water beads.

The light is a spell as it ghosts inside to draw a pointed tall shape. If the floor was snow instead of concrete and if you wanted to make an angel, then this illuminated point could be a wing where your arm now reaches. Now the light wanders the room like a slow star. The wandering shape reaches for the sofa's edge, then further.

You wonder, you're reaching. Leaning you ask, what motion mimics violet?

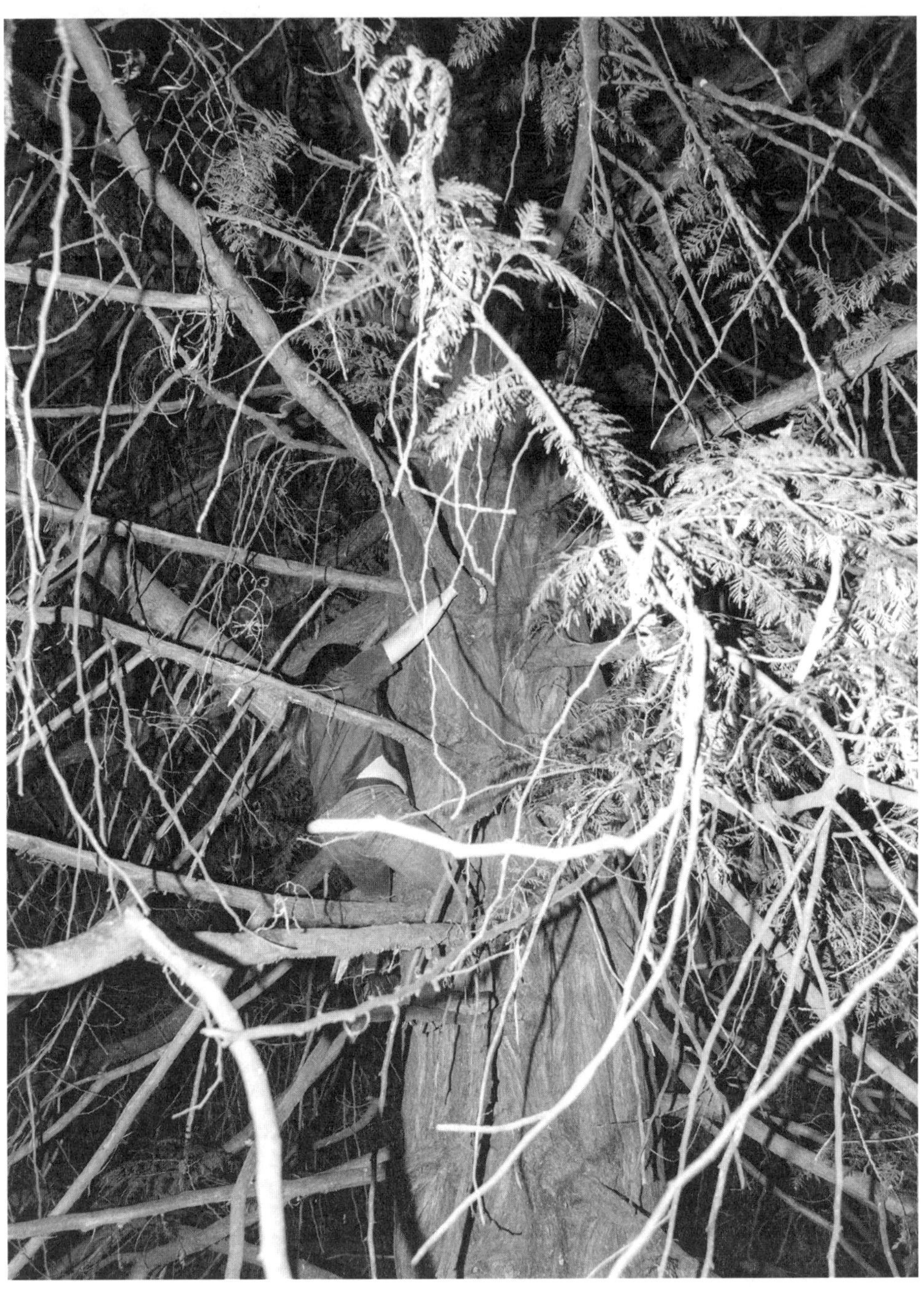

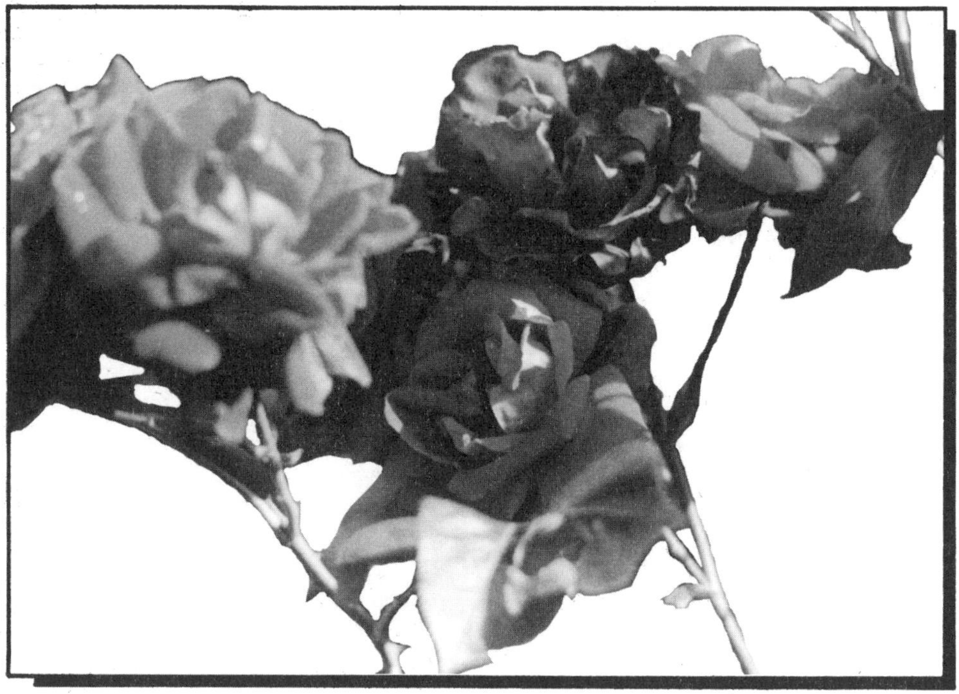

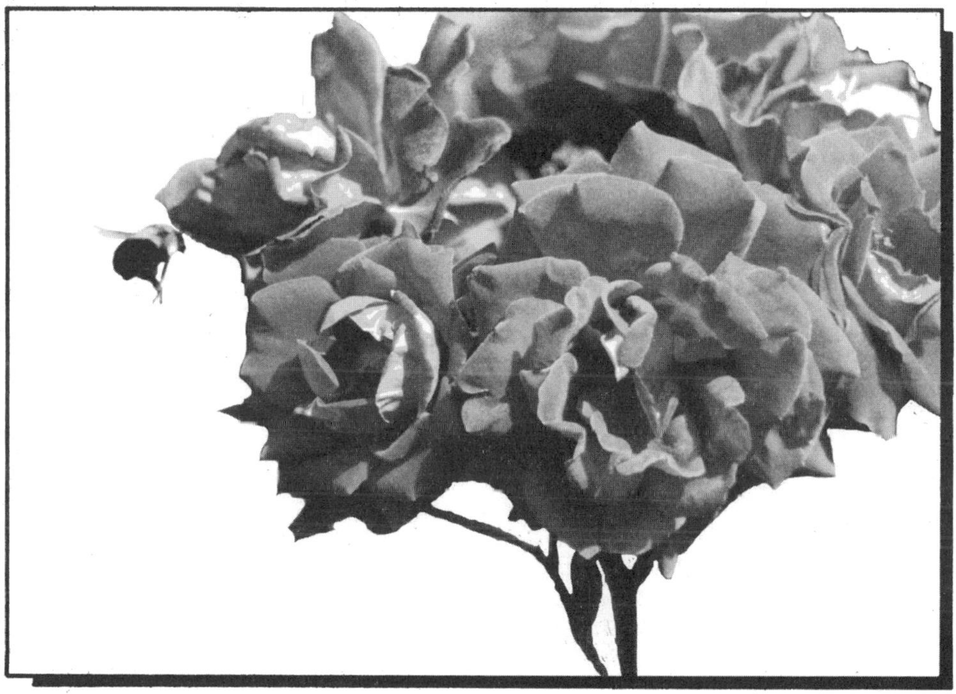

*

I PAUSED TO EXAMINE THE STARS, SOMETHING I DO WITH NO ILLUSION ABOUT UNDER-STANDING.

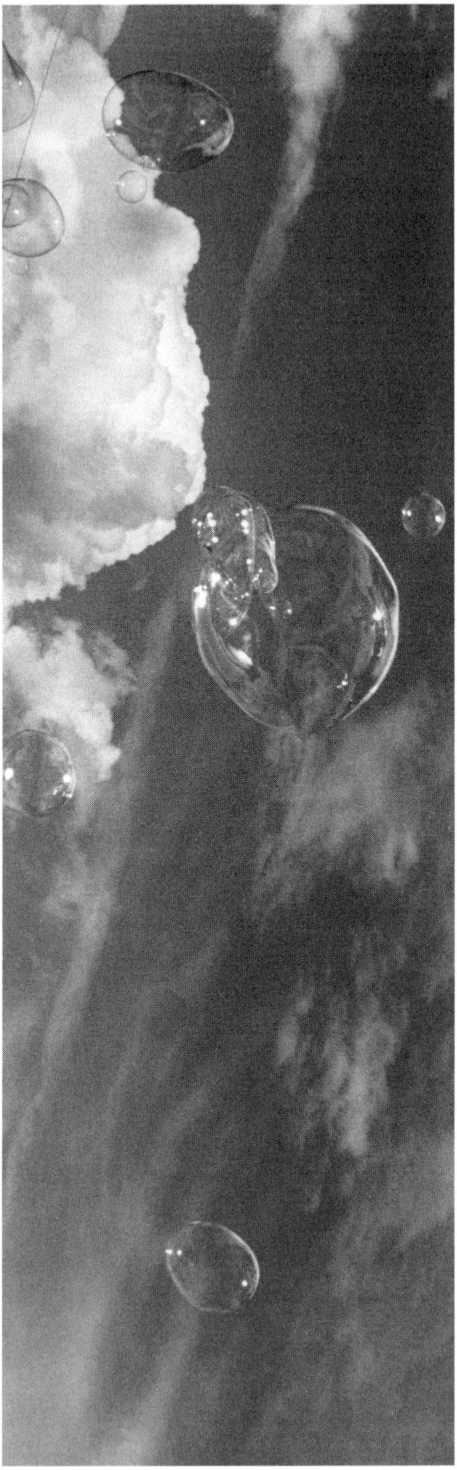

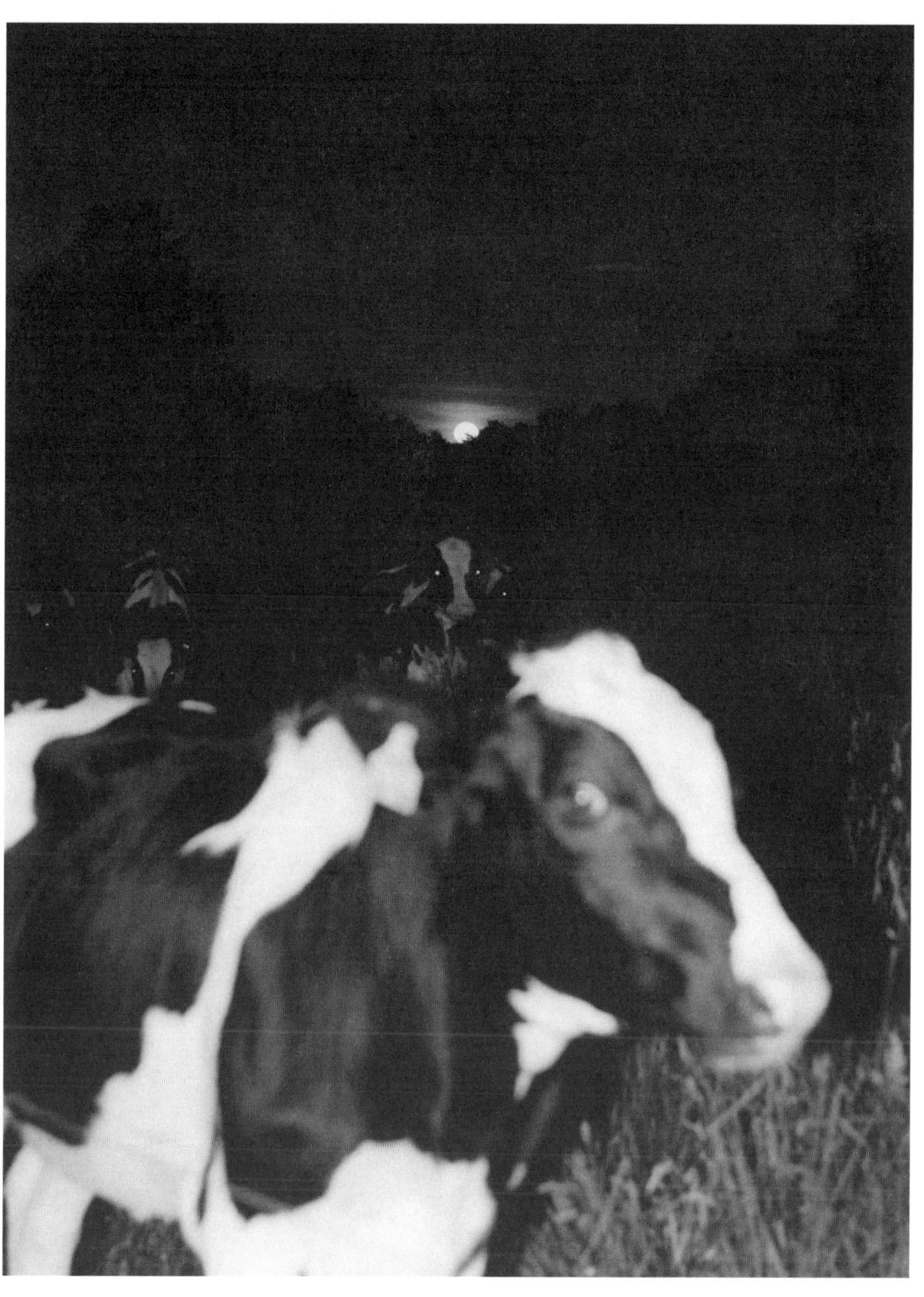

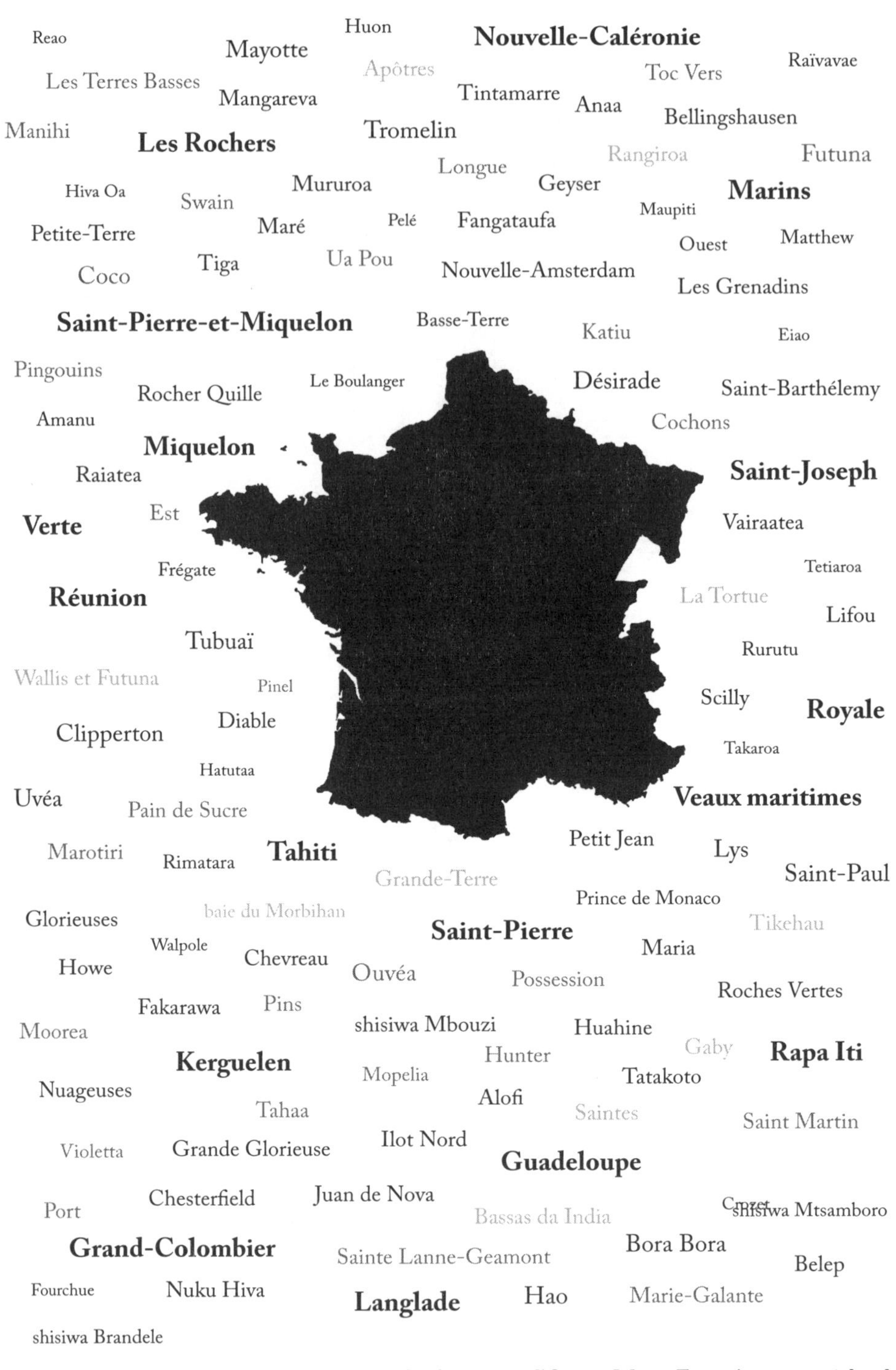

Les îles françaises d'Outre-Mer - France's overseas islands

Martinique

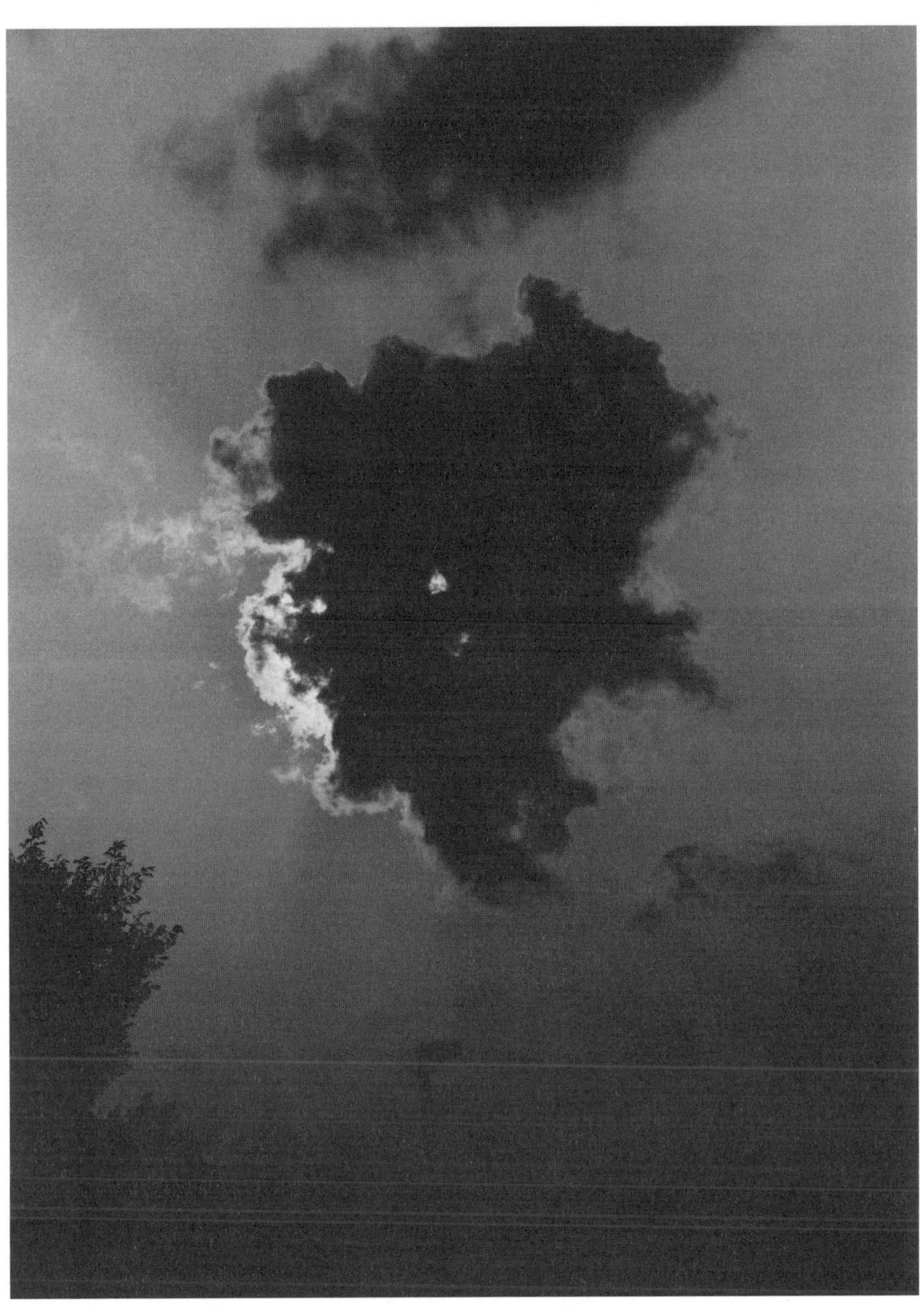

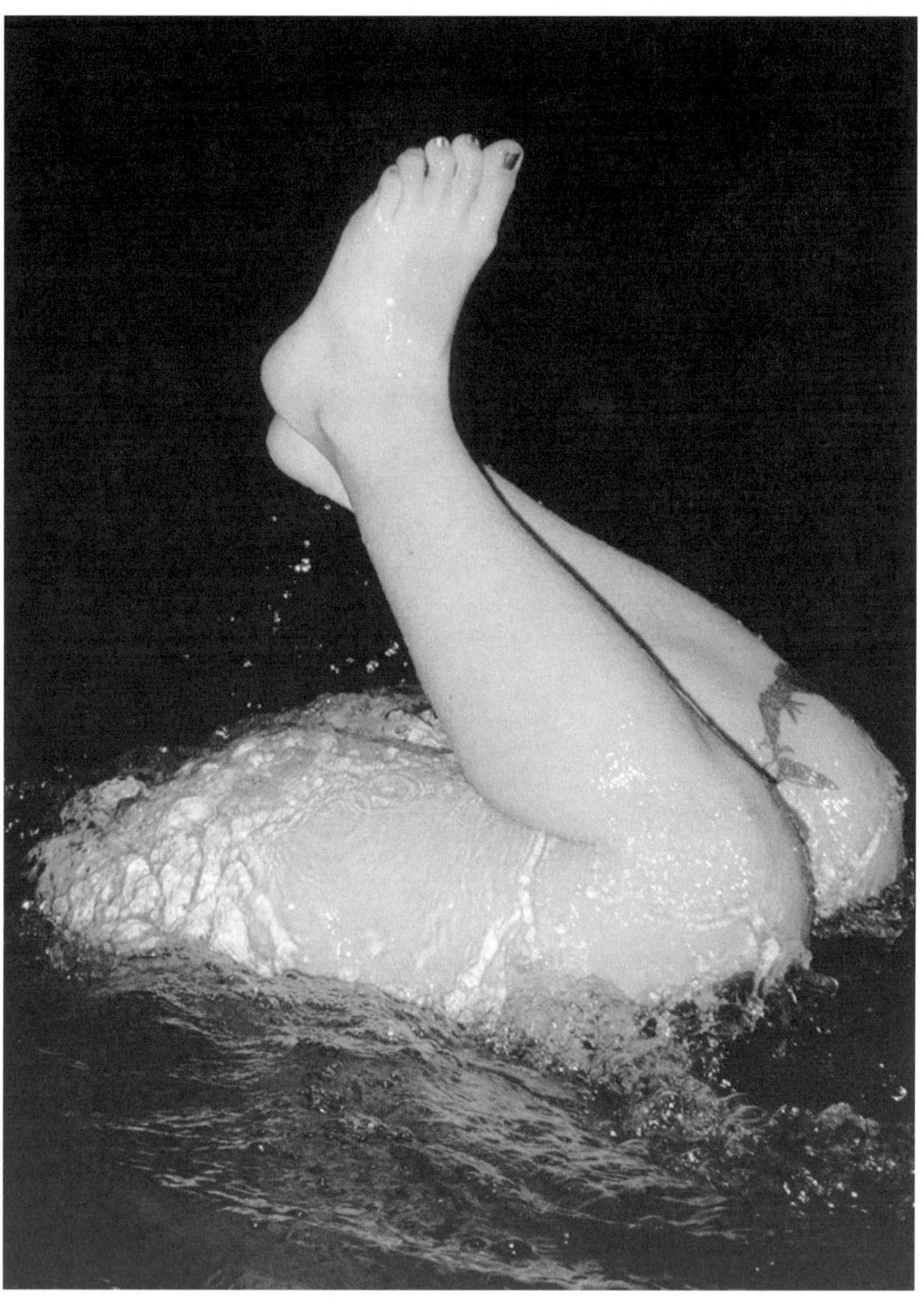

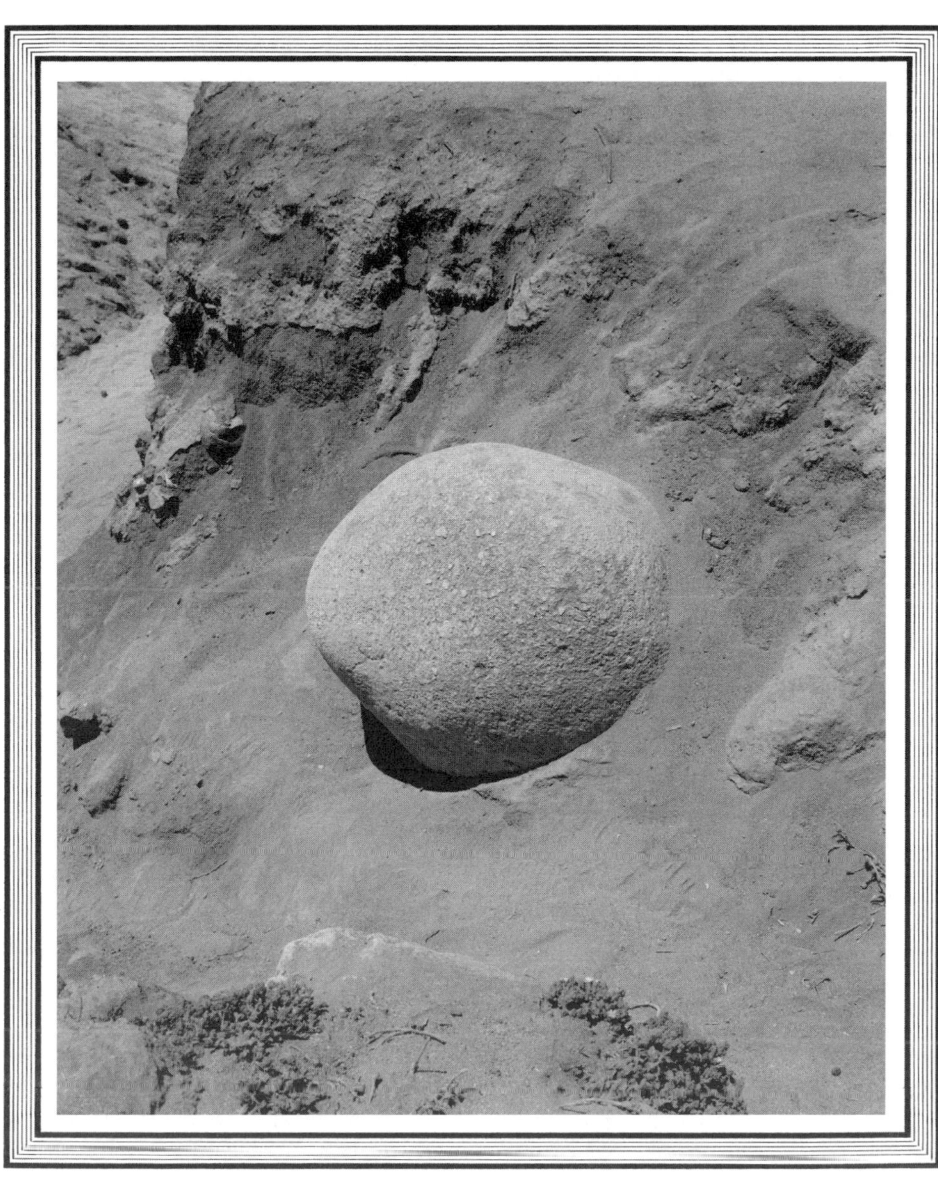

10 THINGS CANCER TAUGHT ME:

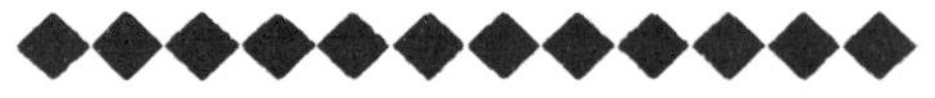

1. **Your ego is useless.**
2. **Most of the things you care about you shouldn't.**
3. **There are things you should care about that you don't.**
4. **Rest is important.**
5. **Cancer is relentless.**
6. **American health insurance is both essential and a complete letdown.**
7. **Capitalism must be destroyed.**
8. **A good shit should be enjoyed; thoroughly.**
9. **You won't be able to remember a lot, like the 9th thing cancer taught you.**
10. **You will die.**

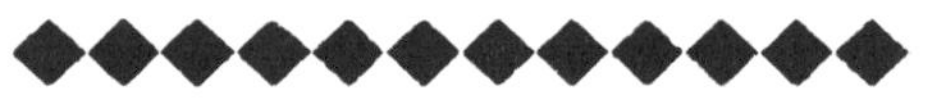

ARE YOU INTERESTED IN THIS PLOT?

My uncle and I don't speak very often, so when I finally listen to his voicemail, I am curious when he mentions he wants to check in. When I call him back, he is just leaving work and answers the call from his car. It's the usual "how you doing conversation" with no real updates. *How are you feeling?* I'm okay. *Have you talked to your mother?* Yes, I just talked to her yesterday. *We talked to her last week, she sounds good.* I mention her memory loss, and he promptly replies, *it's probably because she is still settling in to being back in Israel. Look, it's been a long time since she's lived there.* We all want her memory loss to be circumstantial, rather than an early sign of dementia. This would be a good time to ask him about how he dealt with his father's Alzheimer disease. My uncle is my father's only sibling and the only one left in his immediate family. He has a lot of information I want, and I haven't figured out how to ask. Before I get a chance, he switches topics.

I have a question for you. There is a plot next to your father's in the cemetery—your mother purchased the plot after your father died. My father unexpectedly died from a heart attack at the age of 52. Being 43 years old myself, I finally can comprehend how young he was. *And since it seems like your mother is not coming back to live in the states, I wanted to know if you'd like to have the plot?* Before I answer, he continues, *You don't need to know right away, but I will be retiring next year and then your aunt and I will move to Israel soon after. There will be some paperwork and I can help with that while I'm still here.* I do hate paperwork.

The last time my mother and I visited the cemetery, she said she wanted to be buried in Israel. I had an urge to tell her I wanted her to be buried here, in New Jersey, close enough for me to drive to, but I was unsure if that is something I could ask her for. I said okay and I let the conversation pass.

I guess I have become the next logical candidate for this plot. I am unmarried, a non-parent, and queer, basically a spinster in my family's eyes. Much of my life invisible to them. So, this singular plot situated by my father would not make sense for my brother and his wife who live on Long Island, or my other brother who moved back to Israel over a decade ago. This northern New Jersey cemetery has always been part of my life and now, I have become the heir to this body-sized burial ground.

My grandfather died less than a year after my grandmother and although I don't remember going to her funeral, I do remember canceling my birthday party because of how sick the colon cancer had made her. I can't imagine this memory to be true, but I picture my very young self, standing in the kitchen alone. The large handset of the phone by my ear and the long spiral cord lightly swaying against my body, as I turn the dial on the rotary wall-mounted phone, calling each guest on the list. That was my last childhood birthday party. I didn't want them anymore after that.

When I have gone to the cemetery with my mother, she talks to each of our relatives, gives them a general update, thanks them for what they have given us, and wipes a few tears from her eyes. She will ask me to bring a bottle of water and paper towels from the car. I watch as she pours the liquid from the plastic bottle to wet the stone that has been dirtied with grass clippings and earth that got stuck on the gravestones when maintenance workers mowed the grass. She crouches down to the base of the stone, paper towel in hand, and wipes it clean. I have never seen my mother sob, ever.

My answer to my uncle's question of whether or not I want this plot was, *Probably not, but let me think about it.* He repeats, *Of course, there is no rush. If you do want it, it seems easier to do it while I am still nearby and can do the paperwork.* I am certain I do not want to be buried with my family of origin, in New Jersey, two hours from Philadelphia, my home for almost two decades. But it seemed worth thinking about, because my eyes well up when he asks, because I feel the scattering of bodies across oceans—the further diaspora of this lineage. I wanted to be clear about my decision, or rather, I want to refuse this offer with reason rather than reaction.

After I get off the phone with him, I start to think about my gravestone in this northern New Jersey cemetery. The plot is at the far end of the graveyard, near the chain-link fence that borders the property's edge. I can picture the houses on the other side of the fence, how the grass grows tall alongside it, the narrow pathways between rows, and how there are few trees and no shade in August. My father died in August. We had chosen a black stone for my father's grave. It has a glossy finish that mirrors me as I stand before it, a conspicuous marker against the mostly gray granite slabs nearby. My mother let me and my brothers pick out the stone. Being between the ages of 18 and 24, we thought grey was outdated. Here is what I have for my own inscription so far: "Here lies a queer, who was offered this burial plot that her mother did not want."

Sitting in our backyard later that day, I tell my best friend about my uncle's offer, and without missing a beat she asks, *Won't you be buried next to me?* Everything softens. I relax back into the wood-slatted patio chair and settle into her reminder—we get to live the life we build and not in the life they imagined for us.

I admit I fear being forgotten and I have often thought about who will say Kaddish for the queers who choose not to have children—myself being one of them. I am committed to the idea that parenthood is not the only way to be remembered and as we continue to restructure and rethink family for the living, we also need to complicate the concept of being "the last of the line" and envision how an assemblage of relationships can create a continuous structure. My queerness gives me a different interpretation of family. Our lineage as queers often expands beyond biological ancestors as many of us attach ourselves to queer fore-elders. I think of this act as grafting, creating a different type of family tree, not defined by blood or marriage.

Queers do not come from nowhere. We have ancestry, and we are responsible for one another. How do we honor this different type of lineage, this different type of familial structures? There is a Jewish idea that one's final death is when no one is left to say one's name, and I am concerned that queers without children have been and are less likely to be remembered—I want a ritual for us. A ritual that grants these names existence in this world a little longer, a ritual for the queers that wrote the origin stories of our lives, for the queers those whose mere existence is the origin story of our lives.

There are many Jewish traditions to honor the dead: visiting a gravesite, saying Kaddish, and lighting yahrzeit candles. Years ago, I went to a workshop about creating soul candles, a lost Ashkenazi Jewish tradition where women would make candles to communicate with the souls of their ancestors on behalf of the living. There is little information about how these candles were made. From what I have learned, I picture the women reciting songs or blessings as they walk the boundary of the cemetery where their family members were buried. I imagine one person holding the end of a wick while the other walks unspooling the braided cotton until the string has measured the perimeter of the burial grounds. The women then measure and cut the wick again across the width of a headstone of a loved one. Each cut cord is dipped in wax and twisted together to form sacred candles. We do not know what exactly these looked like, but possibly, each strand of the braided candle represents the soul of a particular person. Since not everyone has access to the burial location of their ancestors, in this workshop we adapted the measurements –measuring with the wick against an object connected with a person, such as a necklace, the rim of a hat, the long edge of a prayerbook, or the perimeter of their photo.

What objects could stand in for those I want to honor?

My mother will eventually be buried in Israel, and I will have to decide what it means to visit her grave. It's upsetting to think about. Ours is a strange and formative relationship. It never settles, but it is a relationship she and I keep showing up to. I have been thinking about what it will mean to give her the honor and to place a rock on her headstone. I think about the land, the stone held in the hand of a Palestinian youth resisting. I am tempted to write that these two moments, my hand placing a stone on my mother's grave and the hand of a Palestinian youth around a stone are entangled, or they happen side by side, or simultaneously, but that would deny the structure of power that exists. The right to visit my mother, during her life or in her death has been given to me against the right of Palestinians to travel and at the cost of Palestinian lives and Palestinian land.

Her move back to Israel means that all our time together is via video or phone calls. She is sitting on her couch, and I am on mine. The way she holds the phone I can't see her entire face, so I am mostly looking at her from her nose up. She has given me a video tour of her apartment dozens of times. It's charming, but it gets old. It never satisfies my desire for connection. She shows me the curtains she bought and hemmed for the living room and where her sewing machine is set up, she goes through the kitchen, uncovering whatever pot she has on the stove, revealing its contents, and points to each and every one of her plants on the porch *—you'll see when you visit*, she tells me. I reply with an affirming nod. I want to see her.

I am not sure if I can do it. I don't want to go to Israel. When I share my hesitation with my friends, they often assure me, *of course, you will visit, it's your mother*. I am not relieved by their assurance, because I know at some point I will.

It is not about seeing my mother; it is about entering the violence; it's about being a closer witness to the complicity. I need no more proof that this injustice exists. I keep asking myself this question about what I do when my beliefs and the ethics of the family I was born into conflict. When I imagine the visit, I imagine the obligation to visit more family. I will go to settlements where my uncles, aunts, and cousins live, on the way I will see the military presence, we will drive

(*continued on page 76*)

Ithaca College

Ithaca 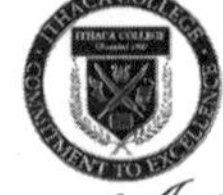 New York

The Trustees of Ithaca College,

upon the recommendation of the Faculty have conferred upon

Eleanor Eichenbaum

the degree

Master of Fine Arts

with all the honors, rights and privileges appertaining thereto.

In Witness Whereof, *under the seal of the College, the signatures of its duly authorized officers are hereunto affixed August 15, 2020.*

La Jerne Terry Cornish, Ph.D.
Provost and Sr. Vice President Academic Affairs

Shirley M. Collado, Ph.D.
President

I chased myself away this summer and when I returned home the apricot trees had died.They bore too much fruit in the springtime when the season was uncommonly wet. Then the clouds ran dry in the hotter months. Still unripe, the copious fruit is seized the moisture away from the leaves and the trees withered.

The tallest of the apricot trees had sent two large, ambitious branches arching over my neighbors fence. In the spring after the summer drought he was the first to point out that the trees weren't budding and appeared dead. He made a point of complimenting the trees and said he was envious of the broad canopy they spread over our yard but his compliments were just a polite and neighborly segue to a request that I remove the trees before the dead branches damaged his fence. I assured him I would work on it the following weekend and I promised to be mindful of the fence.

When I cut the trees, the two branches fell predictably into my neighbor's backyard but the fence was unharmed. By the end of the weekend I had amassed a small mountain of dry, dead wood in my own backyard. Some of the larger chunks I cut and piled for firewood but that still left a heap the size of a minivan that I had to haul around to the front yard where the municipal disposal service would pick it up. When my neighbor saw me dragging the branches around and piling them in my driveway he carried the branches that had fallen in his yard and added them to the pile and then kindly volunteered to help me move the rest.

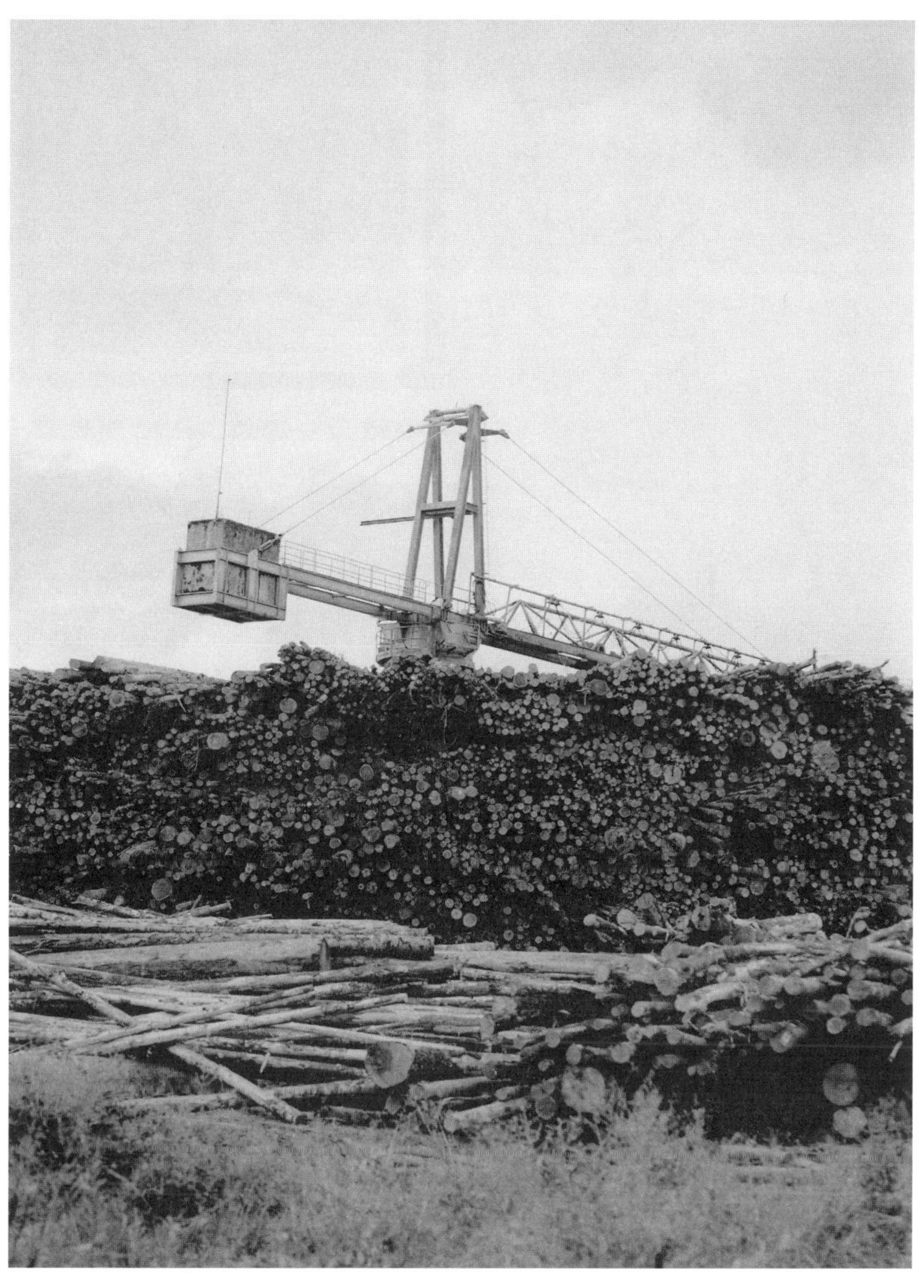

Iluric

AruN

Sein

jUment

Longue

Arz

GavRinis

HoëdIc

Trohennec

GodEc

Les îles de Bretagne - Bretagne's islands

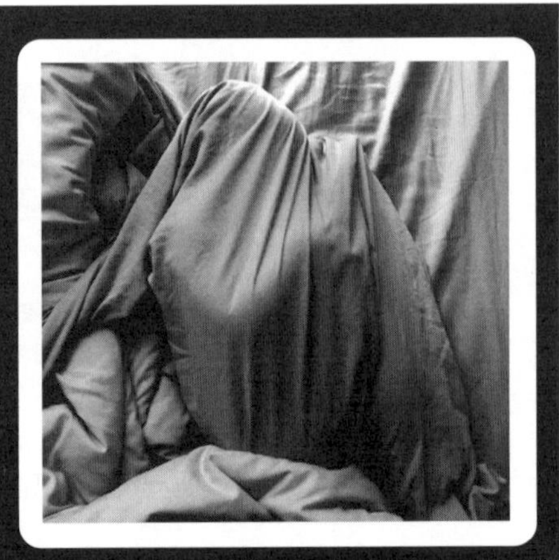

We didn't have much to talk about as we hauled branches around the house and at first we made awkward small talk. After a particularly long lull in the conversation he asked about my wife, "When's she due?" Her second pregnancy was showing quite obviously at that point and it was an easy conversation topic. We chatted pleasantly about children for a few minutes before I naturally asked, "How many kids you got?" I'd always seen kids at his place but I had never counted and couldn't keep track. "I've got seven but two are from my first wife. My oldest, he doesn't talk to me no more. We have three here now, just the twins and Sophie. Our first moved out too and you heard about Natalie."

I had heard about Natalie but it had somehow slipped my mind. I wasn't sure what to say so I just nodded and gave him a sad sort of smile. The conversation fell apart again and we stacked up the rest of the branches in silence.

(*continued from page 4*)

It's going to be ok, he whispered to the moth as he raised it to his eyes. *It's going to be ok*. The doctors had repeated this to him as they raced him to the ICU, charging the defibrillator, as the crash team attempted to stop the convulsions. The look in their eyes, contradicting the intent of their message. People hustled past him as he descended the two flights of stairs, step by step to the street. It was dark, but the sky was glowing from the moisture suspended in the air, capturing the light emitted by the city. Block by block, he maneuvered, careful not to lose the moth, even the most subtle wind would cause the moth to float in his outstretched and cupped hands, suspended below his chin as if he were expecting the sacrament. For such a large insect, it felt weightless, the softness of its body barely registered on his calloused hands. Nearly thirty minutes later they were at his home, in the small yard behind his apartment. He knew there was nothing he could do for the moth, but he wanted to give him a place to rest, to die without being trampled. He assembled a small structure with twigs and sticks in a clearing between the plants. He placed the moth onto the structure with the precision of a jeweler setting a gem. He then sat beside it in the dirt, surrounded by the sticky night, and explained that it would be over soon.

(*continued on page 39*)

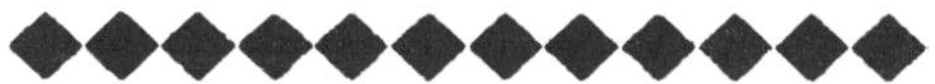

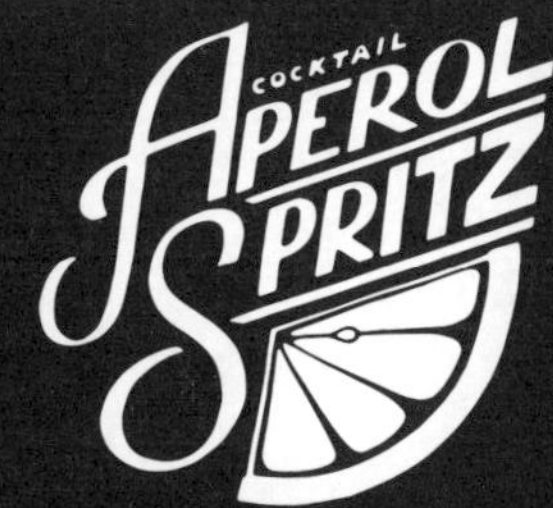

ENTER THE SECRET SPRITZ SWEEPSTAKES

- **Rip a piece of paper into twelve small scraps.**
- **Write one secret on each scrap.**
- **Place one scrap in each section of an empty ice cube tray. Fill tray with water. Freeze.**
- **Pour two ounces of Aperol in a large wine glass.**
- **Top with brut prosecco until the mixture meets midway in the glass.**
- **Drop in ice cubes one by one. You may or may not use all twelve.**
- **Top the beverage with club soda and an orange slice.**
- **Drink!**

You may:

- **Speak your secrets aloud.**
- **Let your secret cubes fully melt.**
- **Photograph them.**
- **Finish your drink and make another.**
- **Practice this exercise on a large scale, with friends. Swap secrets.**

**TO ENTER, TEXT PROOF OF PARTICIPATION TO:
1 (860) 428- 9806**

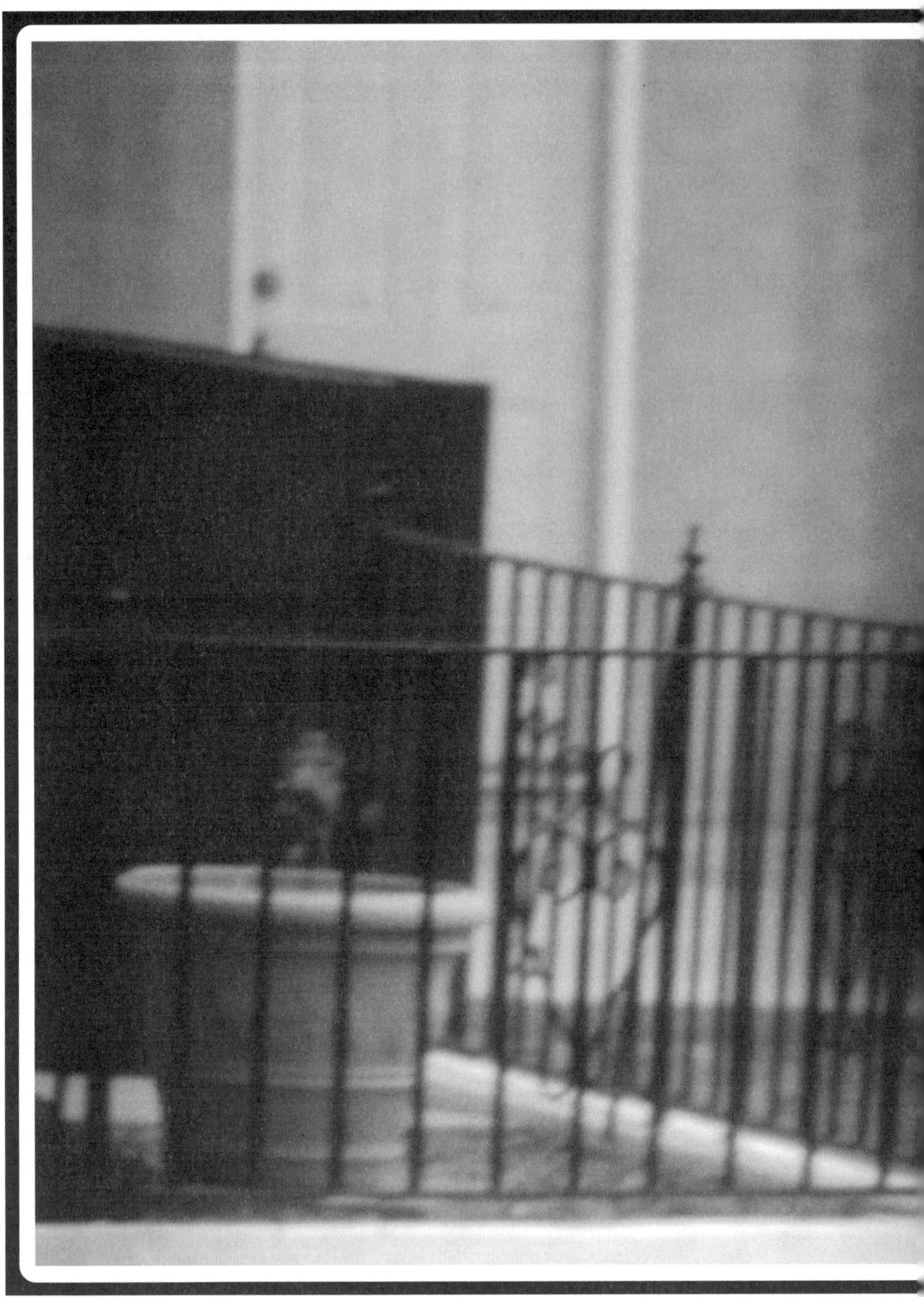

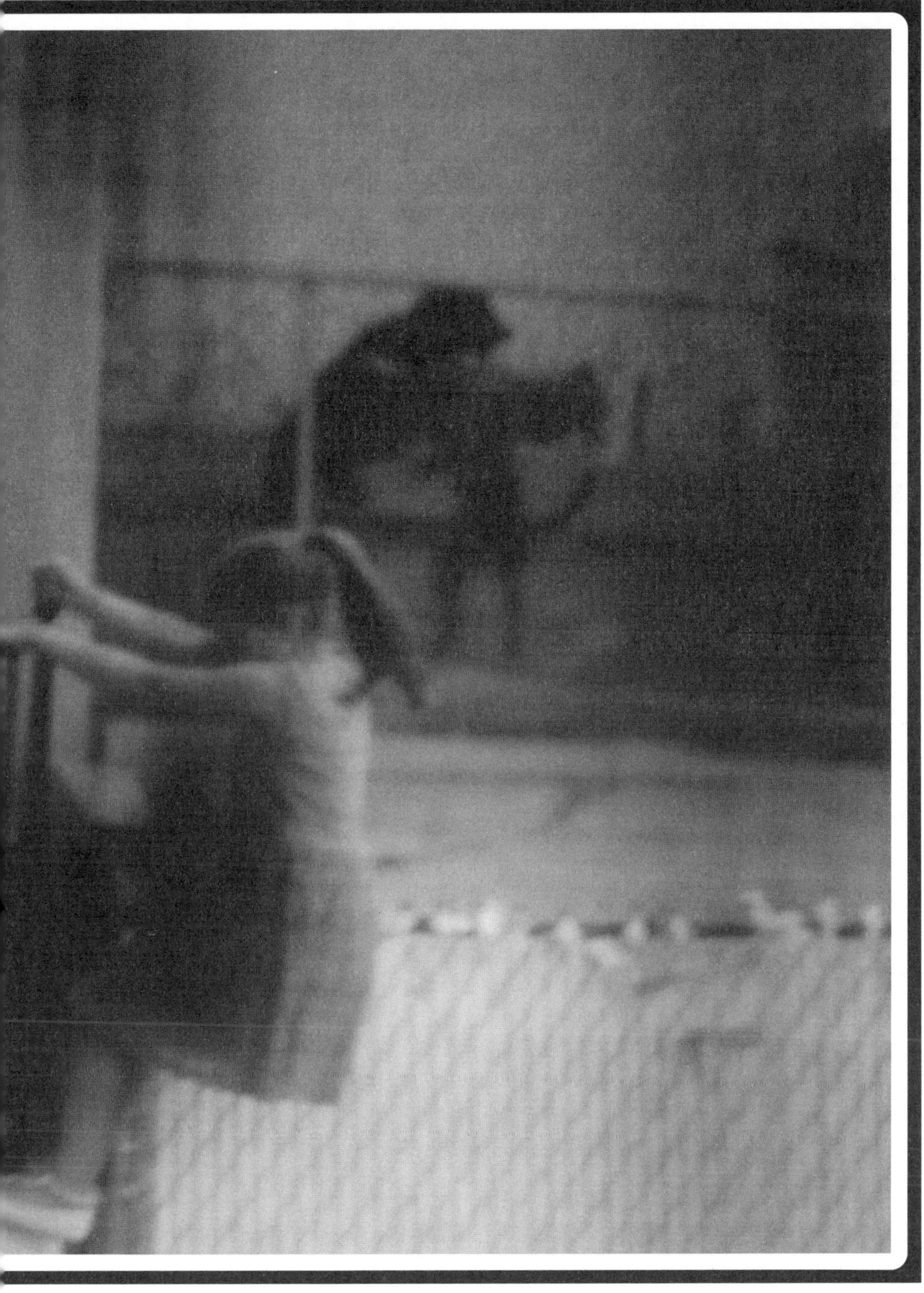

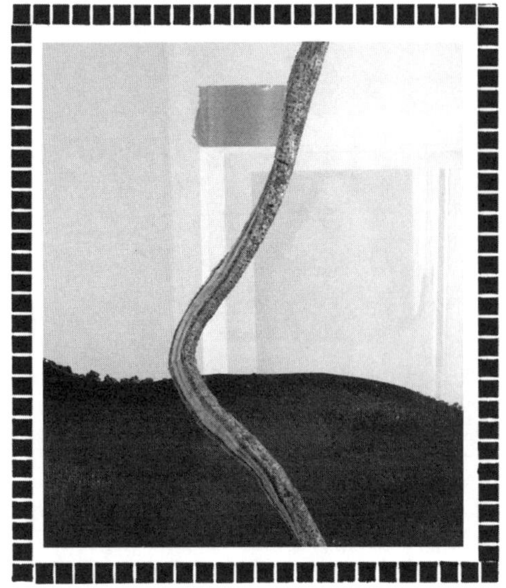

I COME FROM A LONG LINE OF WOMEN WHO GIVE UP THEIR CHILDREN

You have 4 grandparents, 16,384 great, great, great, great, great, great, great, great, great, great, great, great, grandparents. And so forth.

Behind a clear glass vase filled with water
an artist repeatedly arranges Yellow

Red

\+ Purple

flowers.

When I think of my house as an empty vase,
I think of this
\+ water
held in a glass anticipating flowers.

What follows is the memory
of flowers that grew outside my door.
A fuchsia bougainvillea that was beautiful
but raucous with thorns.
When I linger in a memory, that experience of willful
remembering could have a shape. And if not a shape
perhaps
a color: Blue

Gray.

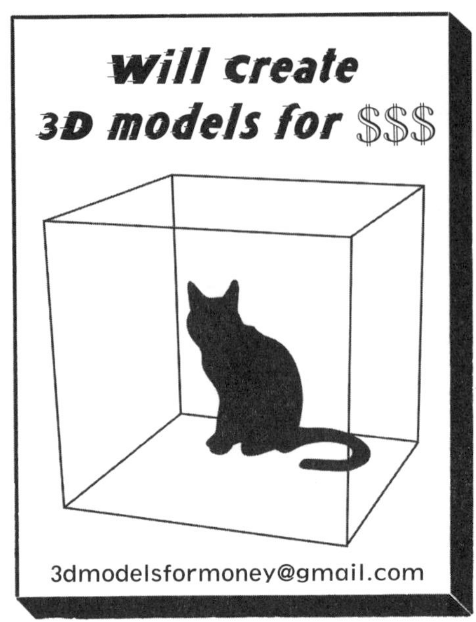

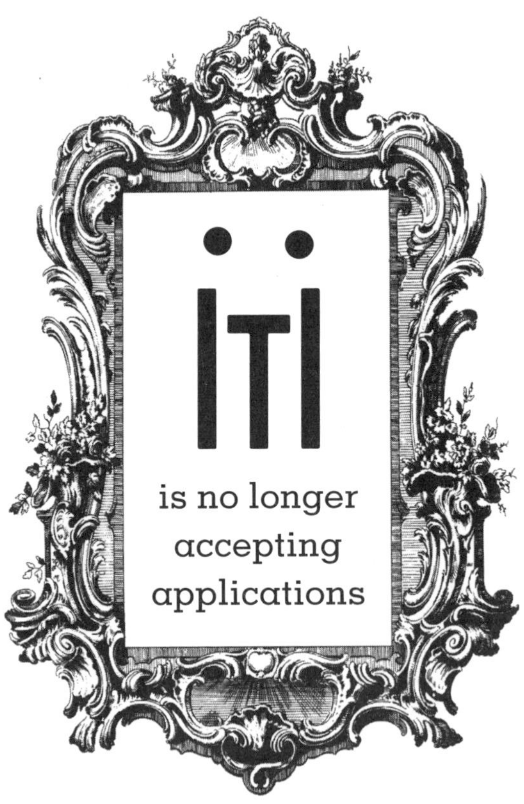

Islands

ParadiSe

RevOlt

SoLitude

Archipelago

DReam

ExilE

L'imaginaire des îles – Islands' imaginary

REEL #3

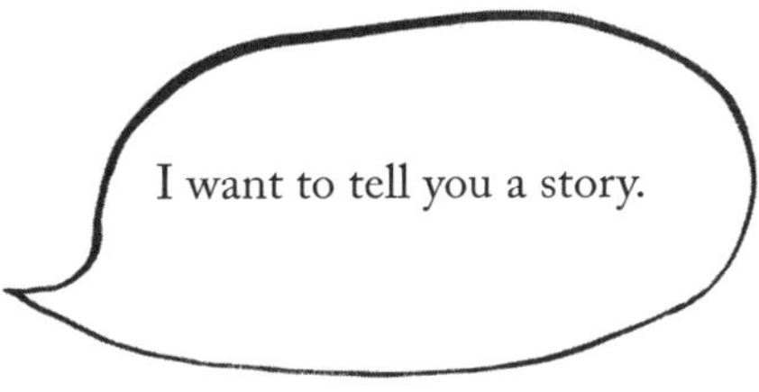

Wait.

It was a long time ago.
Perhaps she said:

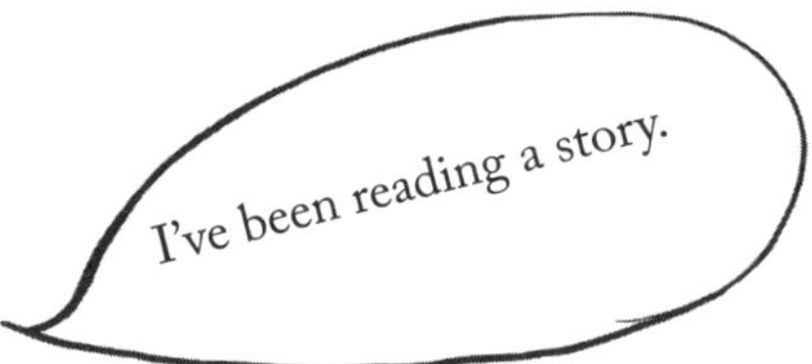

Preserve
Your Memories!

Phone Video to Text Conversion Service
Our team carefully composes a vivid linguistic description from your recorded scene. The final text will detail the video's essence, form, and style. Within 4-6 weeks, you'll receive a printed version of your video in text.

How it works: Email your video (3-minute max per customer) to:
VideoImageInText@gmail.com

$25 per minute of video
(includes transcription and shipping)

This limited offer expires January 2023

After a moment of blackness: the ocean. The horizon is at an angle and the boats are making their way lengthwise. The waves come in their color-tinted neon. The beach is full with everyone at a distance.

A three-hundred-and-sixty-degree rotation, we pan the buildings. We are below, closer to the beach chairs whose legs rest in the sand until we find the sea once more.

She returns, walking towards us, with something clasped in her hands; she is too far for us to make out the object. Her shadow moves from her pointed shoes across the ground. So small you would think the silhouette belonged to a child.

Builders are moving wood from their stacks. All things seem in process, with the exception of one building bearing a bronze plaque turned green by the atmospheric elements of oxygen, rain, and carbon dioxide. We can see the water behind the buildings, the workers stand still.

Back at the ocean. The horizon has straightened itself, more or less. We are seeing what else is around. Sometimes we return to the same place, just to look again.

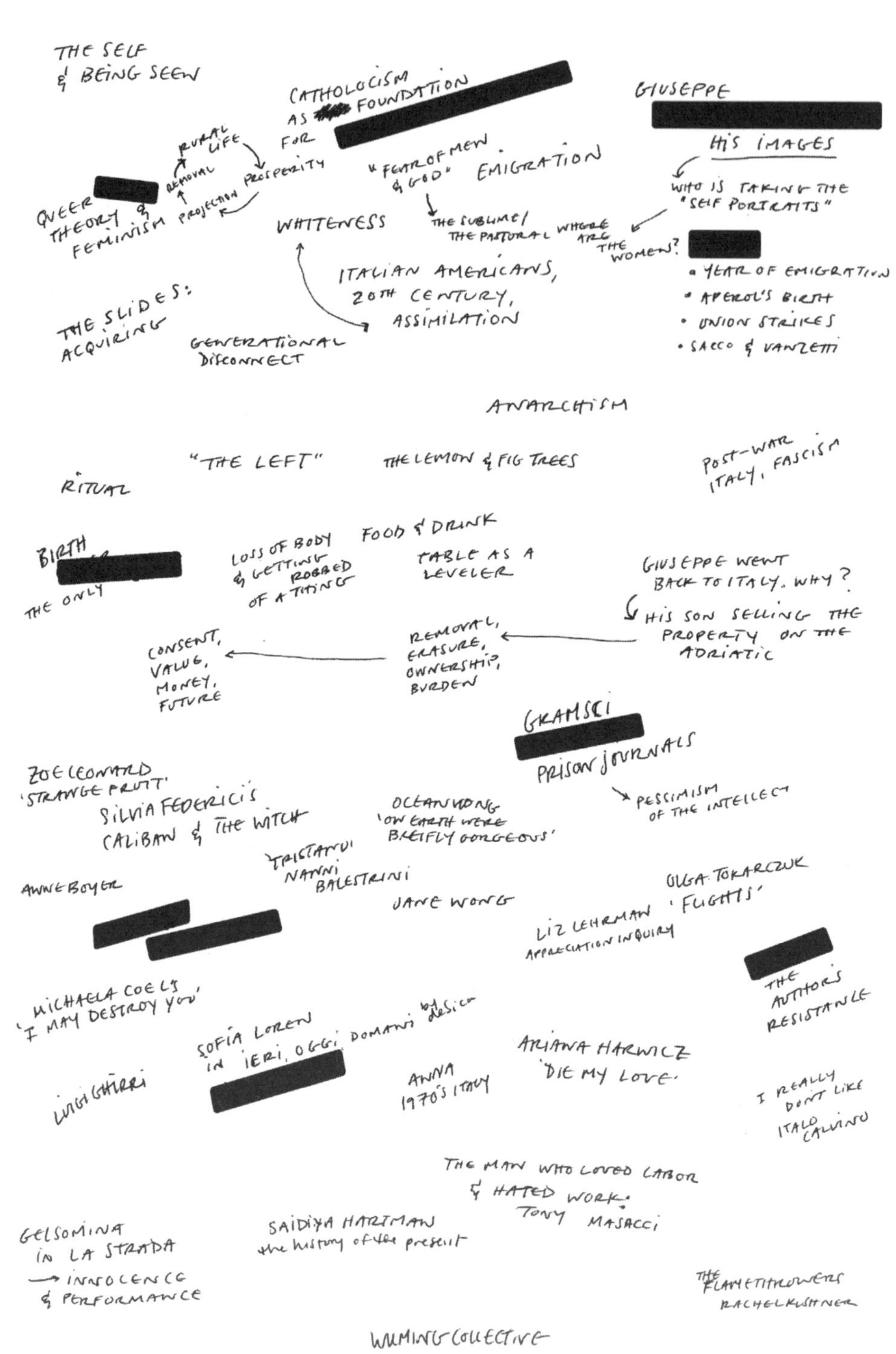
THE SELF
& BEING SEEN
CATHOLOCISM
AS FOUNDATION
FOR
GIUSEPPE
HIS IMAGES
RURAL LIFE
REMOVAL
PROSPERITY
PROJECTION
QUEER
THEORY &
FEMINISM
"FEAR OF MEN
& GOD"
EMIGRATION
WHO IS TAKING THE
"SELF PORTRAITS"
WHITENESS
THE SUBLIME/
THE PASTORAL
WHERE ARE THE WOMEN?
ITALIAN AMERICANS,
20TH CENTURY,
ASSIMILATION
YEAR OF EMIGRATION
APEROL'S BIRTH
UNION STRIKES
SACCO & VANZETTI
THE SLIDES:
ACQUIRING
GENERATIONAL
DISCONNECT
ANARCHISM
"THE LEFT"
THE LEMON & FIG TREES
POST-WAR
ITALY, FASCISM
RITUAL
FOOD & DRINK
BIRTH
THE ONLY
LOSS OF BODY
& GETTING ROBBED
OF A THING
TABLE AS A
LEVELER
GIUSEPPE WENT
BACK TO ITALY. WHY?
HIS SON SELLING THE
PROPERTY ON THE
ADRIATIC
REMOVAL,
ERASURE,
OWNERSHIP,
BURDEN
CONSENT,
VALUE,
MONEY,
FUTURE
GRAMSCI
PRISON JOURNALS
PESSIMISM
OF THE INTELLECT
ZOE LEONARD
'STRANGE FRUIT'
SILVIA FEDERICI'S
CALIBAN & THE WITCH
OCEAN VUONG
'ON EARTH WE'RE
BRIEFLY GORGEOUS'
TRISTANO
NANNI
BALESTRINI
ANNE BOYER
JANE WONG
OLGA TOKARCZUK
'FLIGHTS'
LIZ LEHRMAN
APPRECIATION INQUIRY
THE
AUTHOR'S
RESISTANCE
MICHAELA COEL'S
'I MAY DESTROY YOU'
SOFIA LOREN
IN IERI, OGGI, DOMANI by deSica
ARIANA HARWICZ
'DIE MY LOVE.'
LUIGI GHIRRI
ANNA
1970'S ITALY
I REALLY
DON'T LIKE
ITALO
CALVINO
THE MAN WHO LOVED LABOR
& HATED WORK.
TONY MASACCI
GELSOMINA
IN LA STRADA
→ INNOCENCE
& PERFORMANCE
SAIDIYA HARTMAN
the history of the present
THE
FLAMETHROWERS
RACHEL KUSHNER
WU MING COLLECTIVE

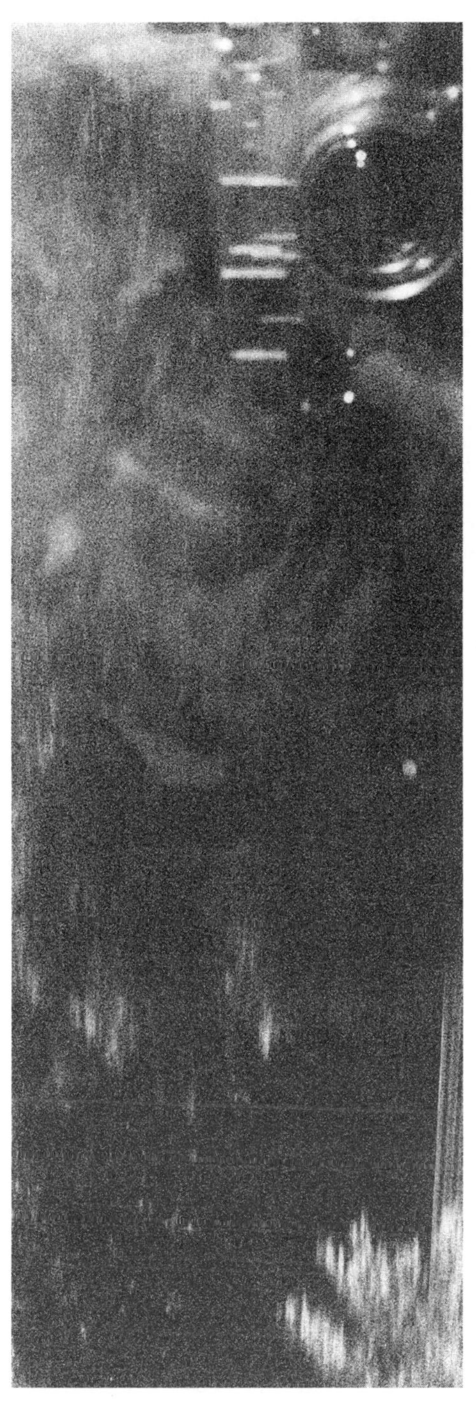

I only knew Natalie's name because she once applied for a job at where I used to work. Not in my department though - I believe she was applying to the receptionist desk and that's where I saw her when she came in. I recognized her and waved casually, she nodded back at me nervously. The woman at the reception desk asked me afterwards, "Do you know Natalie?" That's why I knew her name.

Two and half years before her father helped me with the trees, Natalie and her boyfriend made a ten-hour drive to attend a Las Vegas show, a country music festival at on open-air venue off the main strip. Halfway through the show a lunatic with an arsenal in his hotel suite opened fire

suture
susurre
les mots qui apaisent

les maux
s'immiscent
dans les interstices

glissent au plus profond

rongent de l'intérieur

Many objects hold time. The bottle of sand, the sculpture carved over months, the floor that shows wear, the telephone that tells you how much time you've spent scrolling. As I prepared to move out of my house, I began to find forgotten objects. These tangible things chorused with time and memories while I questioned my gradient of looking.

A peacock feather, notebooks with fragile pages, a jar of shells and shards, some obsolete astrological clippings. Perhaps I mean that I noticed these objects anew.

To escape this scrap chorus, I went outside, into the moonlight. Listening to the calls of frogs and owls, I followed the path of concrete hexagons toward the water. Near the shore, the sky was vast and welcoming as a turned bowl. It was quiet and I paused to examine the stars, something I do often with no illusion about understanding. Three stars in Orion's belt moved across the sky. Minor lights twinkled from the street, but the stars were brighter. Back at the house, I consulted my tattered Pocket Guide to Constellations. The Guide recommended looking for the "Deep-Sky Objects" of Orion Nebula's greenish clouds through a small telescope. Without clouds, it was possible to watch the sky, deeply, but not the deep-sky.

*

Are you tired of being burdened by images?

THE BURDEN OF IMAGES, NEVER WORN

Would you like, instead, to hold my burden of images?

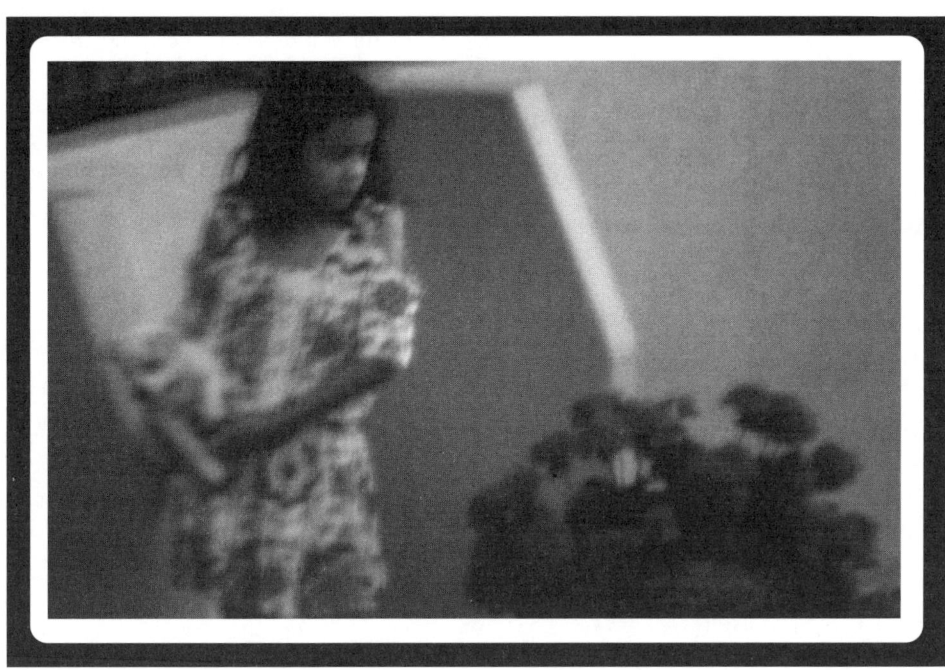

Ithaca College

Ithaca

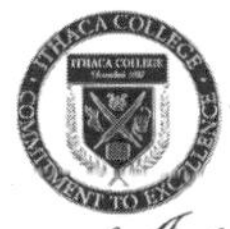

New York

The Trustees of Ithaca College,

upon the recommendation of the Faculty have conferred upon

Will Fujio Walters Matsuda

the degree

Master of Fine Arts

with all the honors, rights and privileges appertaining thereto.

In Witness Whereof, *under the seal of the College, the signatures of its duly authorized officers are hereunto affixed August 15, 2020.*

La Jerne Terry Cornish, Ph.D.
Provost and Sr. Vice President Academic Affairs

Shirley M. Collado, Ph.D.
President

The picture as a telescope, a binocular, a kaleidoscope. A challenge or an altar for my vision. A shift in understanding, memory storage, a vacuum-seal—to hold water or to be held. It wants to look elegant, maybe graphic, to be a gram of a photogram, a part of a larger scatter, one side of a long constellation. It speckles over a backdrop. I think of my brother pointing at the three dots on my right cheek, *Orion's Belt*, he'd say, *A Hunter*. Is this thing full of only negative space, of wonder, of refusal, of a dried stalk of lavender given to me by a friend? *It only smells when you step on it*, she said. Pictures work that way too. We can only see them when we look, then look away. Or when we digitize and de-digitize and crumple them up and avert our eyes to somewhere else. We only see a picture when we see it elsewhere. We only see ourselves when we see ourselves elsewhere.

from his window on the 32nd floor across street from the concert. Natalie and her boyfriend both bolted as the crowd began to panic and scatter. They managed to stay together as far as the street outside the gate where Natalie was wounded and collapsed on the asphalt. Her boyfriend tried to stay with her, hold her hand and flag down help but they were separated by emergency personnel. She was still breathing when first responders pulled them apart and ushered him and other still-ambulatory survivors into a sheltered storefront and barricaded the doors. He was still clutching the small purse she'd asked him to hold during the concert and her phone and ID were inside the purse.

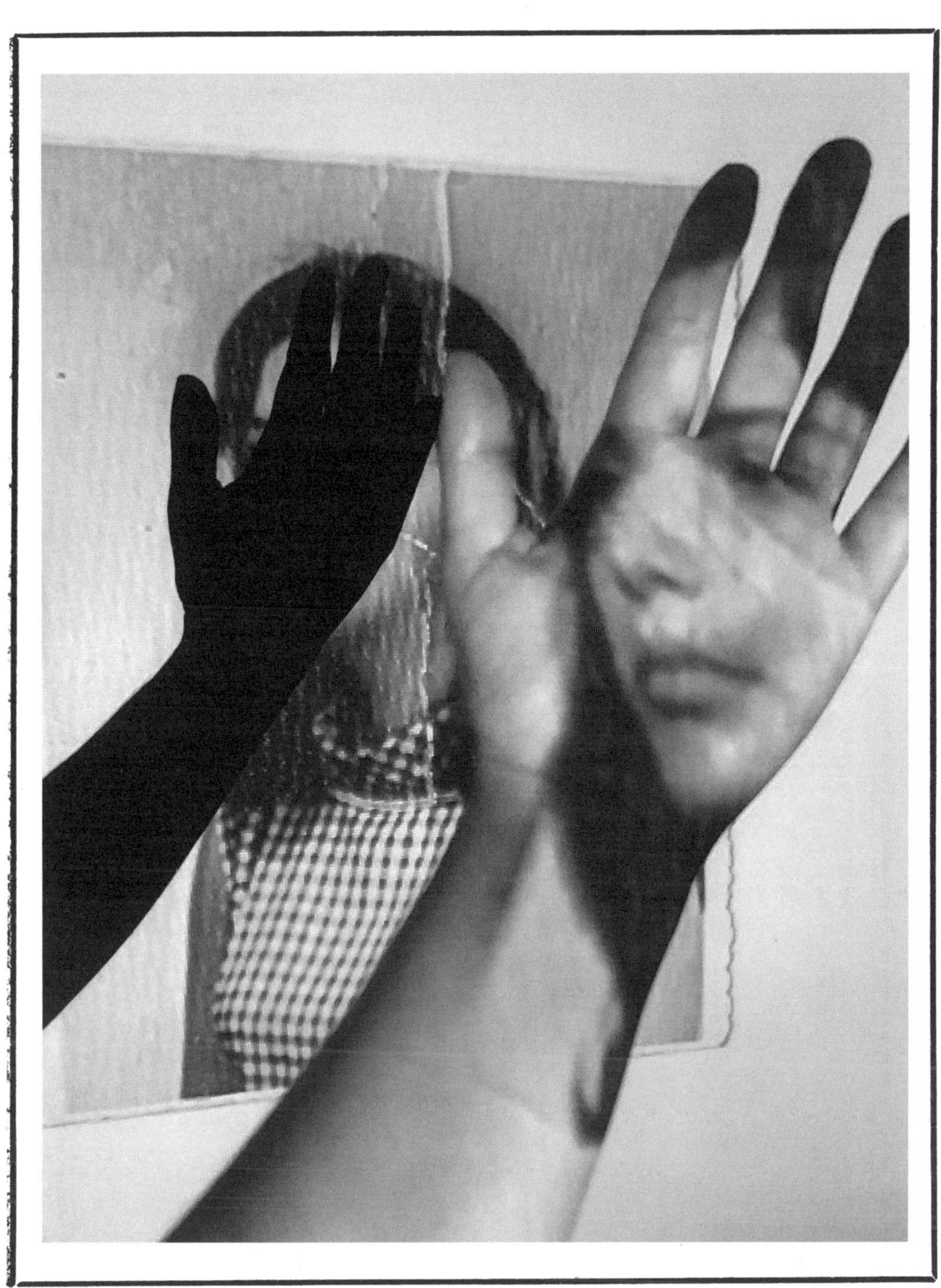

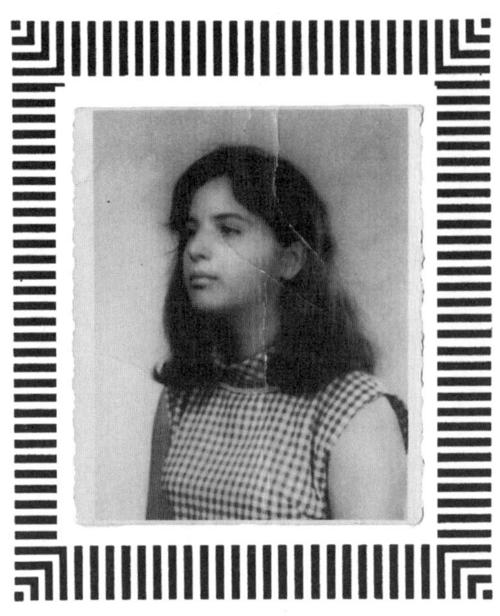

mère qui envahit l'espace
efface les traces

à chaque marée
recommencer

noyée l'espérance

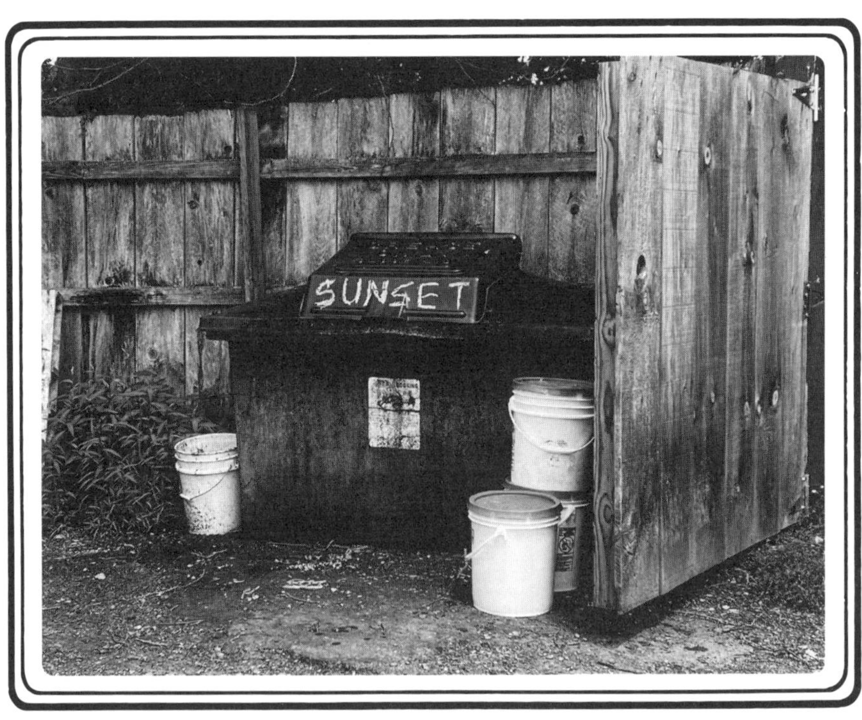

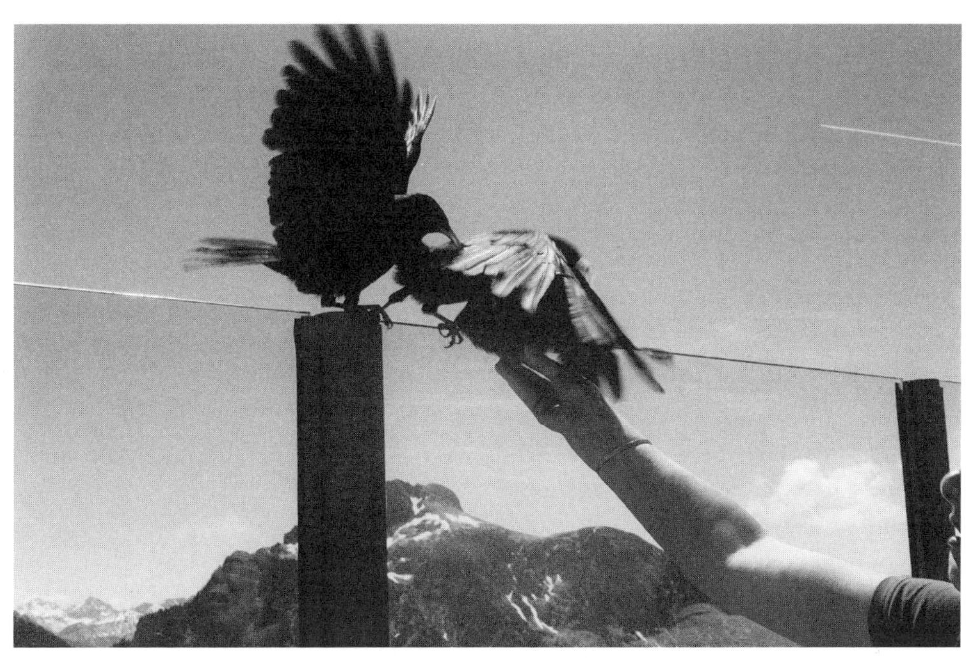

Ithaca College

Ithaca

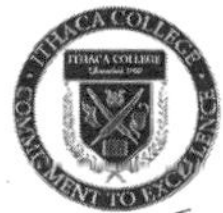

New York

The Trustees of Ithaca College,

upon the recommendation of the Faculty have conferred upon

Marissa Lamartino

the degree

Master of Fine Arts

with all the honors, rights and privileges appertaining thereto.

In Witness Whereof, *under the seal of the College, the signatures of its duly authorized officers are hereunto affixed August 15, 2020.*

La Jerne Terry Cornish, Ph.D.
Provost and Sr. Vice President Academic Affairs

Shirley M. Collado, Ph.D.
President

Sometimes when I wake up, I am startled to find that the crust around my eyes has hardened into crystals. Hard and jagged, like gravel eyeliner. I think of my body as a soft thing—jelly contained by skin. On mornings like this I am reminded of its minerality. On sweaty days my skin looks like a topographic map with contour lines of salt.

I don't consume hard things for the most part. I eat a lot of yogurt. This leads me to the conclusion that my body is a machine whose purpose is transforming soft things into hard things, which squeeze out of my pores like an otter pop while I sleep. The body at rest is capable of incredible things.

When I die, I imagine that the little bits of rock and mineral that remain in my body, the precious metals that my body has converted so beautifully, the heavy metals too, will just sit there, while the rest of me fades away.

Sarira, which comes from the Sanskrit word for body, describes the crystal remnants that remain after a corpse is cremated. Buddhist monks will sift through the ashes of their saints and teachers for these little stones. Rather than a remnant of the body, they are seen as a distillation.

According to Buddhist records, 200 years after Buddha's death, King Ashoka, who united most of the Indian subcontinent, collected some 84,000 of Buddha's sarira, and stored each one of them in separate pagodas spread as far as Thailand and Japan. Having that many gems inside your body must be uncomfortable, loud, and rattly. It makes me wonder what it would sound like if you tipped the Buddha upside down.

It is said that sarira will multiply for those who deserve them. King Ashoka must have been doing something right. Conquesting and empiring doesn't seem righteous to me, I have to admit, but I don't have any sarira of my own, so who am I to say? To clarify, I am writing to you from the position of someone who has not received any sarira, which appears to be something different from producing sarira from one's own body. I would have to be burnt to a crisp to know for sure, and I haven't gone through with that yet.

I learned to care for rocks from my maternal grandparents. They spent their weekends driving three or four hours to remote areas in Oregon known for their geodes and crystals. After digging around in the high desert's loamy soil, they collected and bagged the bits of Earth, which they later categorized according to the specific ways in which the material had been assembled through various combinations of time, pressure, and elements. I love rocks, but I don't know them very well.

A mineral is a naturally occurring inorganic element or compound having an orderly internal structure and characteristic chemical composition, crystal form, and physical properties. Common minerals include quartz, feldspar, mica, amphibole, olivine, and calcite.

A rock is an aggregate of one or more minerals, or a body of undifferentiated mineral matter. Common rocks include granite, basalt, limestone, and sandstone.

This definition, provided by the United States Geological Survey, tells me rocks are chaotic and minerals follow rules. To know a rock you must know its structure and its history in relation to the Earth. And more importantly, you must know a pebble's relation to the universe—where its contents originate. I find it frustrating that inherent in the word "geology" is the focus on the Earth with the use of the latin root "geo." Other bodies in the universe have geology too, and none of that material has any relation to the Earth. I'm not sure that even the physical material on Earth has anything uniquely Earthy about it. It is just where this stuff is located in space right now. It wasn't here in the past and it won't be here in the future. Taking care of rocks is no different than keeping flowers in a vase, which is why I keep them both on my desk. The objects embody fleeting moments in time, the only difference is scale.

LIGHT IS A CUTE
FORM OF ENERGY
OF COURSE IT
WOULDN'T OVERPOWER
A BLACK HOLE!

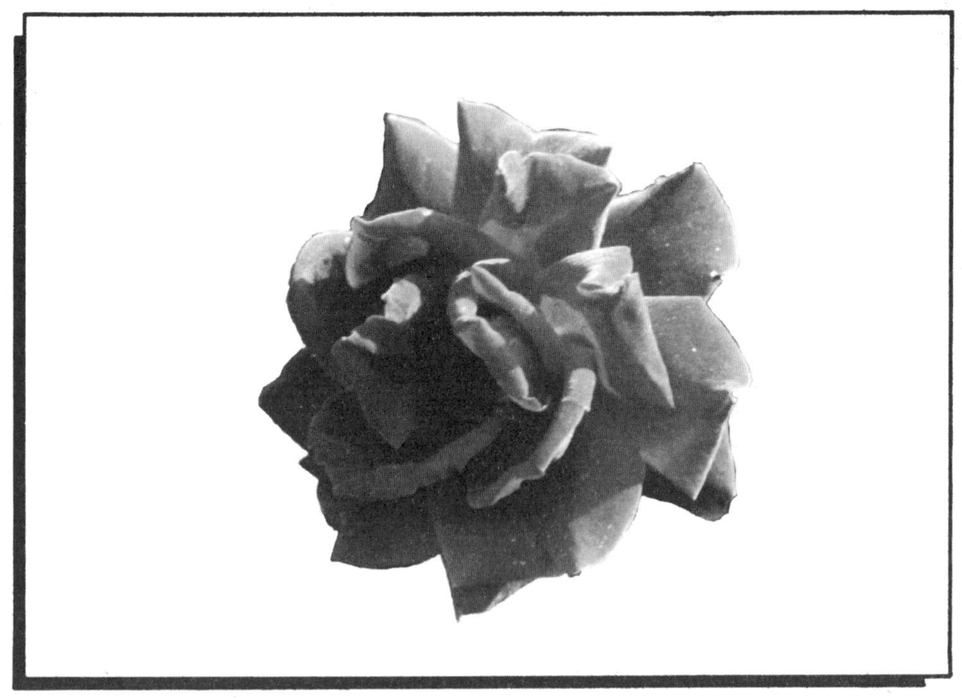

Ithaca College

Ithaca 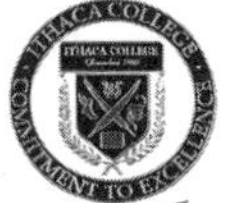 New York

The Trustees of Ithaca College,

upon the recommendation of the Faculty have conferred upon

Erika Alexandra Morillo Echavarría

the degree

Master of Fine Arts

with all the honors, rights and privileges appertaining thereto.

In Witness Whereof, *under the seal of the College, the signatures of its duly authorized officers are hereunto affixed August 15, 2020.*

La Jerne Terry Cornish, Ph.D.
Provost and Sr. Vice President Academic Affairs

Shirley M. Collado, Ph.D.
President

THE GLOWING
BLUE LIQUID DOES
LOOK DELICIOUS...

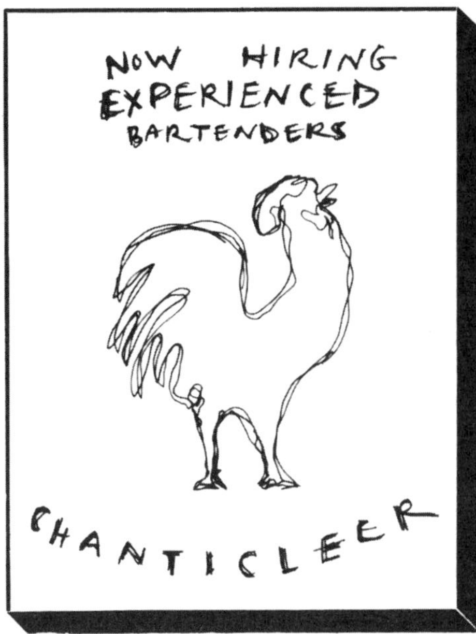

The day I was born, Russian astronauts prepared for long term space living. And what is long term? I ask, the days feeling both long and short.

Would you like to hear about a picture I saw?

Send me a postcard with your return address to:

P.O. Box 34582
San Diego, CA
USA 92163

& I will send back a letter about a picture I saw.

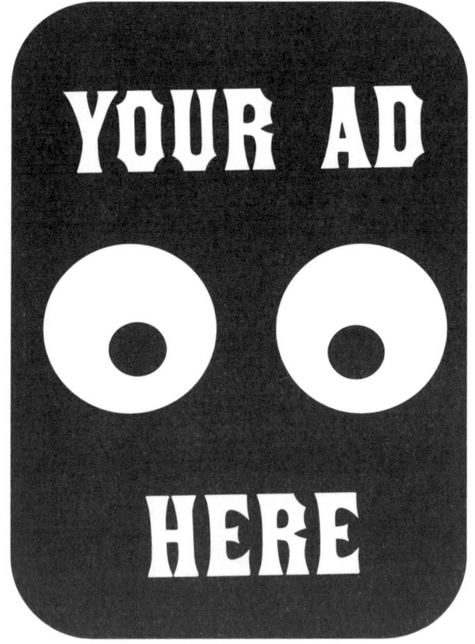

(*continued from page 19*)

He laid in bed worrying about the moth, eventually falling into an uncomfortable sleep. As the summer light broke through the bedroom window he quickly got up and went to check on the moth. Hoping with each step that it would be gone, allowing him to believe he had saved it. As he approached, he saw the moth was still on the handmade perch and it appeared to be moving. This was good he thought, great even, but as he kneeled in the dirt to get closer he noticed a river of ants emerging from the ground, rushing up the twig structure and engulfing the moth like fire on a burning home. He watched for a moment in awe of the sheer violence nature permits. He grabbed the moth from the stilts and placed it on the ground, said I'm sorry, half choking up for what he had done, raised his foot in the air, paused for a moment to ensure his angle was right, and drove his foot straight down as if he were trying to crush something far deeper in the earth. He repeated this action as the moth and the ants were eviscerated in a manner as brutal as the one it was ending. He stood there blankly with death emerging from the edges of his shoe.

So Natalie was unconscious and unidentified when they rushed her blindly to one of three frantic emergency rooms all across the city. It was almost two days before her family knew for sure that she hadn't survived.

The students at the local high school held a candlelight vigil for Natalie the evening after the shooting. Natalie had graduated less than two years before and clearly had been popular there. Several hundred students, faculty and other people in the community gathered in the school parking lot. They cried and hugged one another and took turns telling stories about Natalie from an improvised stage in the bed of someone's pickup. Before the evening was over, the vigil had spontaneously transitioned into a fundraiser for an on-campus permanent memorial that eventually manifested in a kind of gazebo built by the junior shop class. The gazebo surrounds a concrete birdbath with a mournful, miniature angel statue in the center. A brass placard on the gazebo has Natalie's name, birth year and death year marked on it. The flagstones that formed the foundations of the memorial have already gone askew.

Tomorrow will be three weeks since my daughter was born. It was a scheduled delivery about five days ahead of her official due date, my wife's doctor said that there was some kind of blood flow restriction in the umbilical cord that made inducement necessary. The flow apparently was diminished by two to three percent, not anything to raise

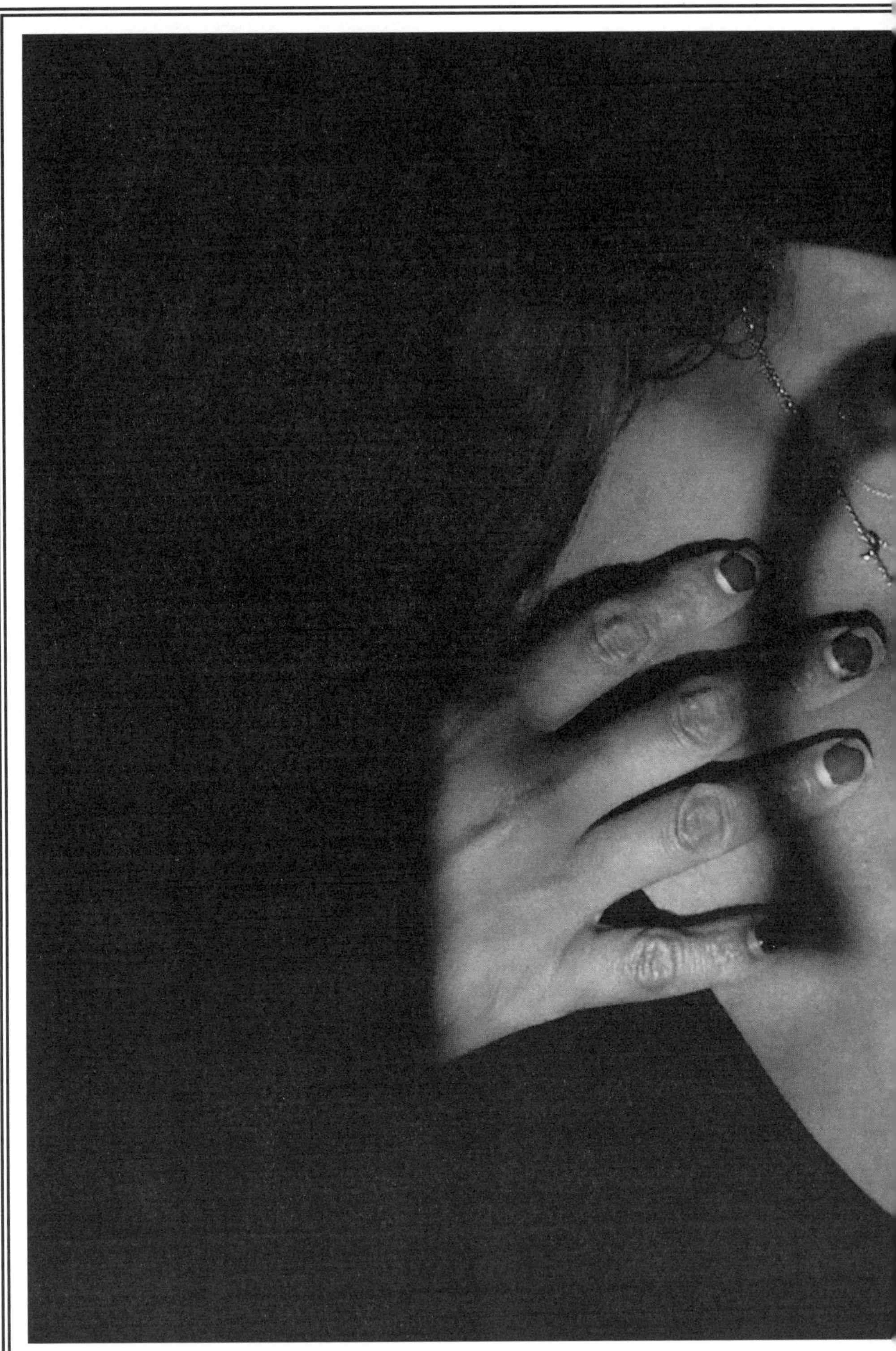

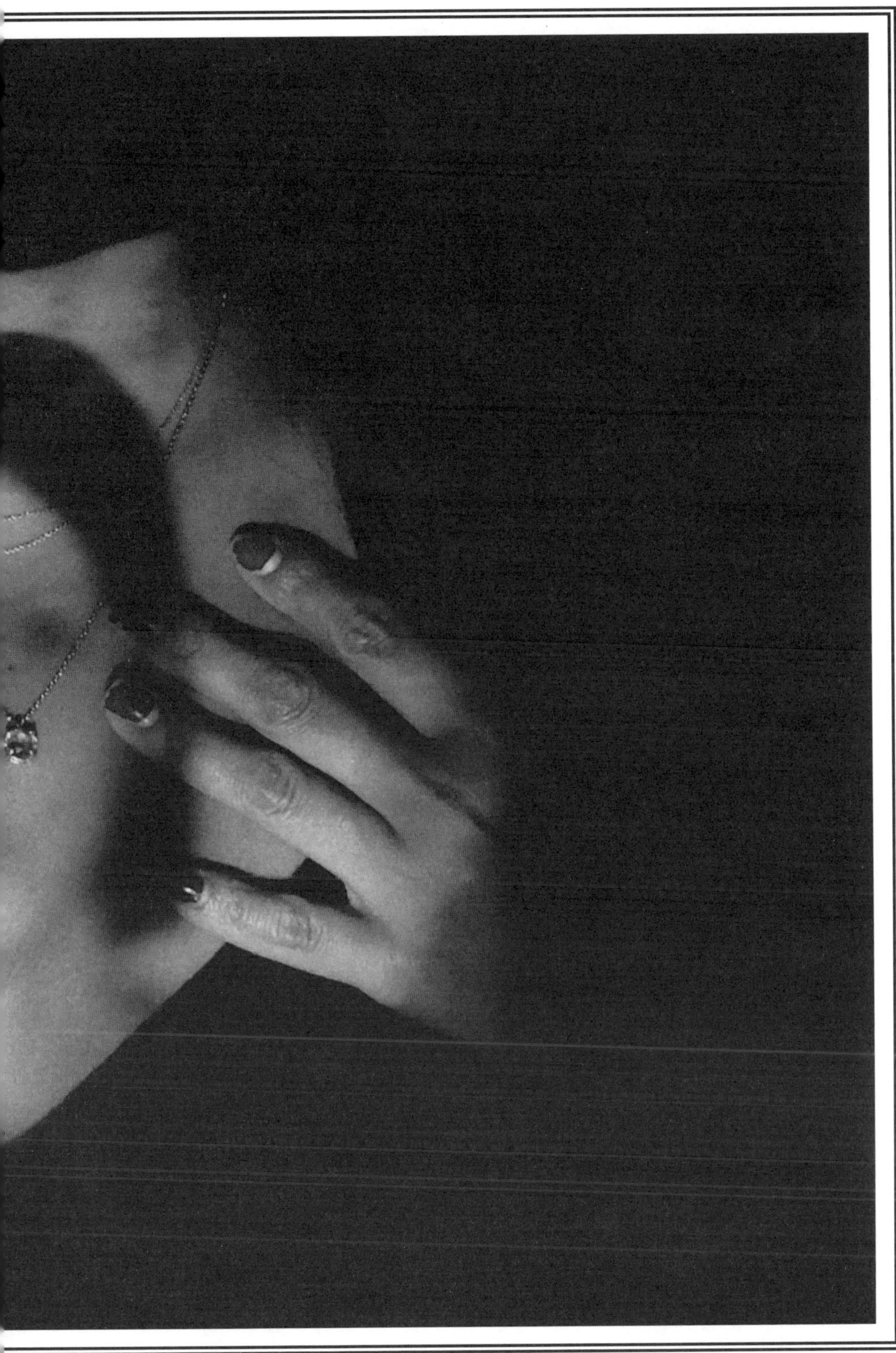

A silk fountain is a trick in which the magician reveals layers of vibrantly colored silks from a closed hand. The silks pile impossibly on top of each other in a cascade of spilling fabrics. On the internet, magicians chat about how this trick delights the crowd in excess, in drama. The trick hinges on impossibility, but it is a trick of folding.

To see, to believe.

I think of folding paper and of opening and closing doors. I think of fans and folding screens. The intentional bending of a plane creates function, and someone makes a choice.

To begin a paper fortune teller, first fold a square piece of paper in half, diagonally, both ways. Unfold the paper and then fold it again to create opposing seams. The seams become guides, as you continue opening and folding the paper in quadrants. The paper is embossed with its history of folding.

To create the game, stretch the folded paper to fit the hands. When the game is played, the player makes choices. Eventually, the player's fortune is revealed. The unknown, cast from a sheet of paper, produces wonder.

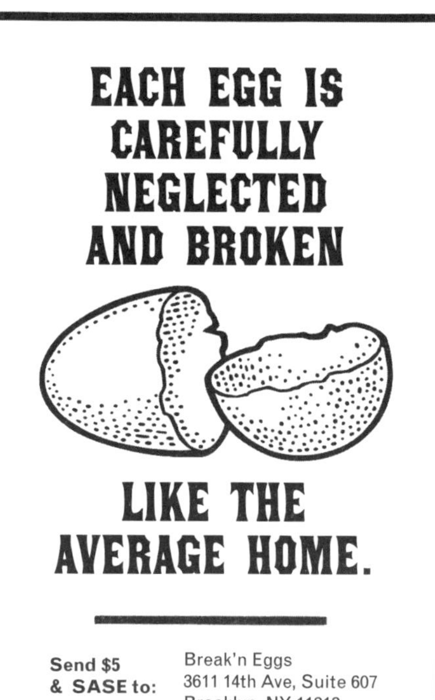

A SHORT LIST OF PICTURES

- Someone holding a wooden seagull
- Deer sniffing an oil spill on the road
- Graffiti:
  IF GOV'T WON'T HELP WHAT IS IT FOR?
- Blurry gemstones nestled in a red bandana
- A FaceTime dinner
- A circle of men holding their balls, and only their balls, outside the tops of their jeans
- A postal truck on its side, middle of road
- A man in a button-up shirt with a snake climbing up his chest. I thought it was a tie.
- A baby, slightly older

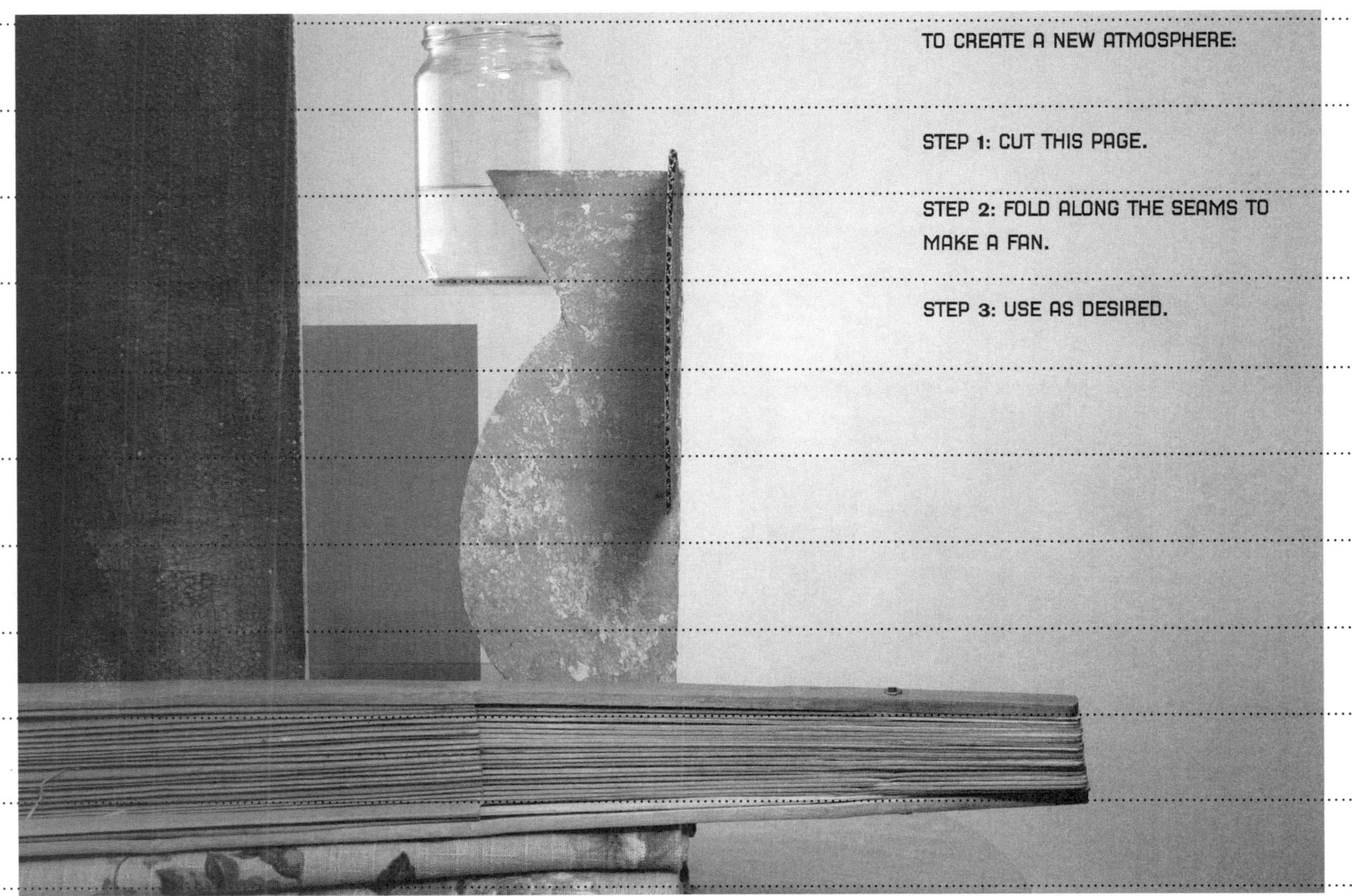
TO CREATE A NEW ATMOSPHERE:
STEP 1: CUT THIS PAGE.
STEP 2: FOLD ALONG THE SEAMS TO MAKE A FAN.
STEP 3: USE AS DESIRED.

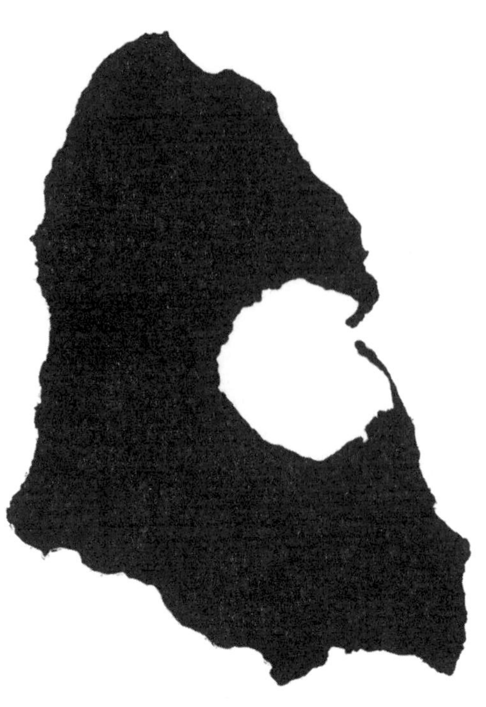

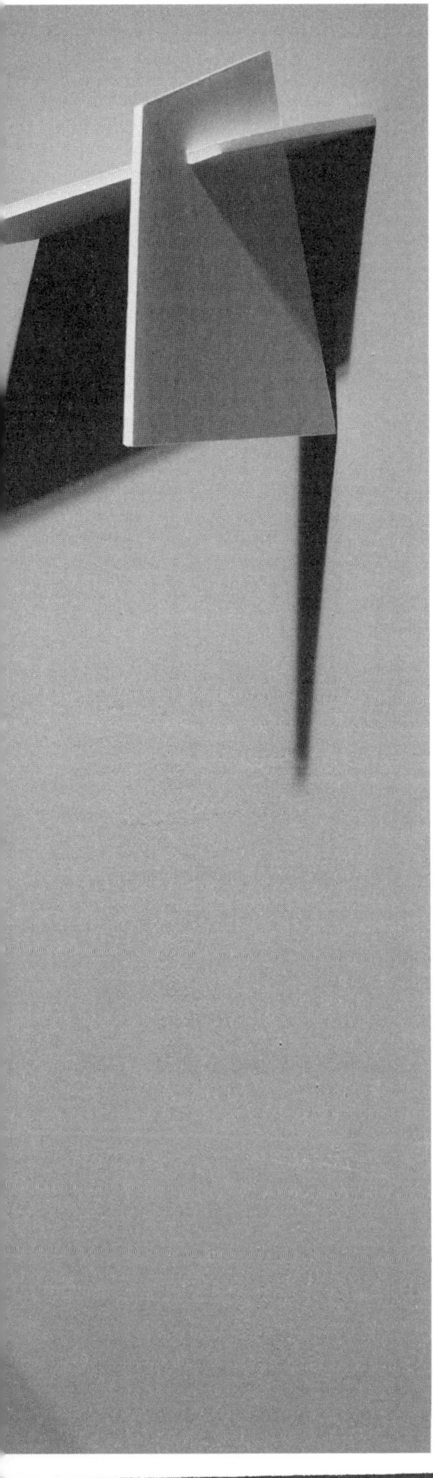

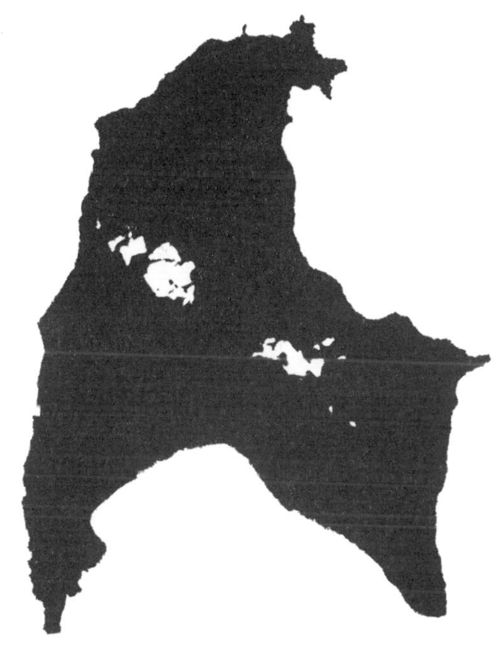

Ithaca College

Ithaca

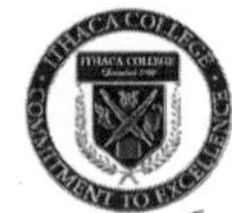

New York

The Trustees of Ithaca College,

upon the recommendation of the Faculty have conferred upon

Michael Popp

the degree

Master of Fine Arts

with all the honors, rights and privileges appertaining thereto.

In Witness Whereof, *under the seal of the College, the signatures of its duly authorized officers are hereunto affixed August 15, 2020.*

La Jerne Terry Cornish, Ph.D.
Provost and Sr. Vice President Academic Affairs

Shirley M. Collado, Ph.D.
President

se reconstruire
sans elle
malgré elle

se reconstruire et apaiser
la colère
diffuse
comme
les
racines
restées
sous
terre

My small scale photo theft currently amounts to a single medium ivory box, filled mostly with cheap glossy prints, a few kodachrome and ektachrome slides shot by my father, and some old black and white images bent into cylinders. This one photograph, however, I did not have to steal.

What did my body do when I was hit by that car? What did my body rearrange into? Who did I become? What happened to me? There is no footage, no image. I do not know what happened to my body. Do I only know what happens to my body if it is something imaged? I want to know how I lay. I want to know how the fuck you leave someone you might have killed in the middle of the road on their back, how you make eye contact and then continue on with your day. Did she cry after? Was she upset that I might have fucked up her car? Does she know what I look like? I was wearing a mask, hand sewn with ribbon and floral fabric by a stranger on the Upper West Side. Does she think about me? Texas plate, red sedan. Body left in the middle of the road, two imprints of the bolts of her license plate. A month later I lose hearing in my right ear for ten minutes. On the drive out to California, Jeremy nearly hits a deer on I-80, driving at least eighty, and somchow the deer zig zags and does not die, and neither do we. The deer, today, is better at this than me. My body did not move like that. My body ended up on the ground, and after a few seconds I was there with it. The sun was so bright. The only thing she touched was my thigh. I did not want to go after her. That deer avoided a car at eighty miles per hour and I could not avoid one at ten. But Jeremy tried to stop the car and the woman who hit me, the Texan, did not.

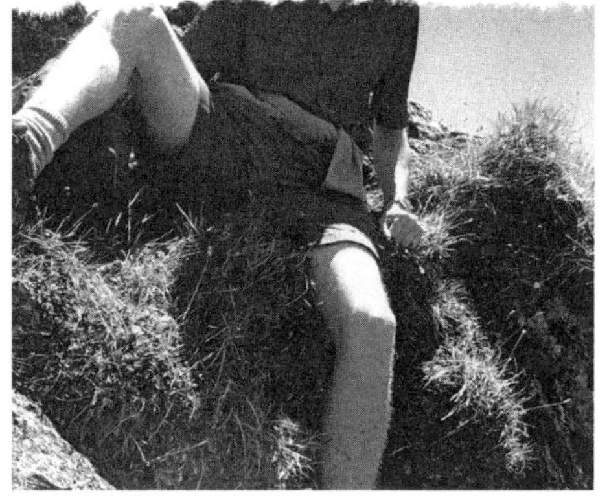

DOESN'T IT FEEL NICE TO WRITE SOMEONE A LETTER?

DOESN'T IT FEEL NICE TO RECEIVE A LETTER FROM SOMEONE?

THIS IS AN ADVERTISEMENT BY ME FOR THE POST OFFICE.

Things I am old enough to remember: different seasons. Apples need frost, says the new Jenny Offill book. I remember frost. I remember frost, and the first warm day in March and getting my feet wet in the bay, and then the first warm day moved up to February, and then it was warm in December and warm in January and when it is always warm who's to say what the first warm day is? And the way it got cold, which was different. I remember a cool September. I remember summer nights that felt cool. I remember my first hurricane, which happened just before I turned six, and I remember the one that felt apocalyptic and took out all the traffic lights and flooded the neighborhood, and then of course I remember the one fourteen months later, which was actually apocalyptic and left my mother without power for twelve days but without fish in her living room, unlike the people across the street, which she described with pride, as though it were a personal success rather than horrible luck and the way that our house, which sat at the bottom of a sloped street, was the only one in the entire neighborhood not in a flood zone. I remember wearing a jacket to the book fair the first time I went, and how three years later I wore a thin-strapped leotard and pants, shoulders bare, hair shorter and just grazing said bare shoulders.

I remember snow. I read an article about snow days that does not describe how they are becoming rarer here in New York City. I remember snow in April nearly May; April 17th, the parking lot of my building a foggy lake outside my plate glass window, and how two friends who lived in the building crowded into my room looking out, as though we could see anything other than ourselves in the reflection. I remember a very warm February first, during the beginning wave of my mother's surgeries, and how I drove the car to the backside of Cheesequake Park and snuck in through a broken fence; we mostly did this in summer to avoid paying the entrance fee, but in the quasi-spring of February I just didn't want to see anyone else. My shoulders were bare then too.

I remember shaving my armpits in the shell-shaped sink so that no one would see the hair there. I remember Eric telling the person who undid me that he had seen the sprigs of pubic hair above the waistline of my jeans and that I needed to get rid of it. I remember my body being policed and who policed it—my mother, my father, boys at school, doctors, everyone had a say in my body—and I remember spring, and cherry blossoms, and how you could do the same thing at the same time every year because of the seasons, and how they seem almost completely gone now, how some of my flowers bloomed in November and some bulbs are pushing up now in February. How the gardening subreddit I look at, there are people posting their magnolias for Valentine's Day and someone comments, Can't say it isn't real now, huh? These are supposed to come up in April. I remember my mother's magnolia in the front yard, and her dogwood, and the deadness of March, and the comparative vibrance of April, the shiny pinkness of it, the gentleness of it.

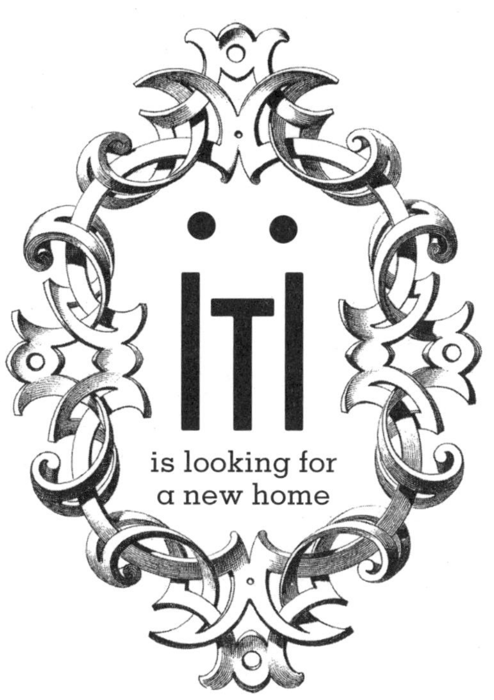

les mots qui ne veulent pas sortir

bloqués

au fond

de la gorge

gorge qui pourrit

ne laisse plus passer

les flux nourriciers

les mots

alarms but it was less than optimal and it was inhibiting her growth. My wife's mother had flown in to help with the new baby, she spent some fourteen hours shrouded in a mask, gloves and face shield to navigate the airport network and she was still on state-mandated quarantine in the downstairs bedroom on the morning I dropped my wife off at the hospital. She scheduled her flight to deliberately give her quarantine time before the due date but that was before the doctor decided to move up the delivery. The same mandate that kept my wife's mother in isolation prevented me from going with my wife into the hospital. We had spent months asking whether I'd be allowed into the delivery room and every doctor had a different answer. The shifting and uncertain situation surely made their protocols irregular. Ultimately, it didn't really matter what the hospital rules were or what her doctor said because, with my wife's mother still downstairs, we had nobody else to stay with our son. My wife and I loaded up our son and an extra, empty car seat and her bag that she'd packed for a planned four-day stay in the hospital. We shared a cup of coffee as I drove and then I dropped her off in the parking lot with a kiss on the head and a good luck pat on her belly.

I took the long way home so I could listen to the radio and clear my mind. I felt like I was somehow failing as a husband and a father. I remembered from

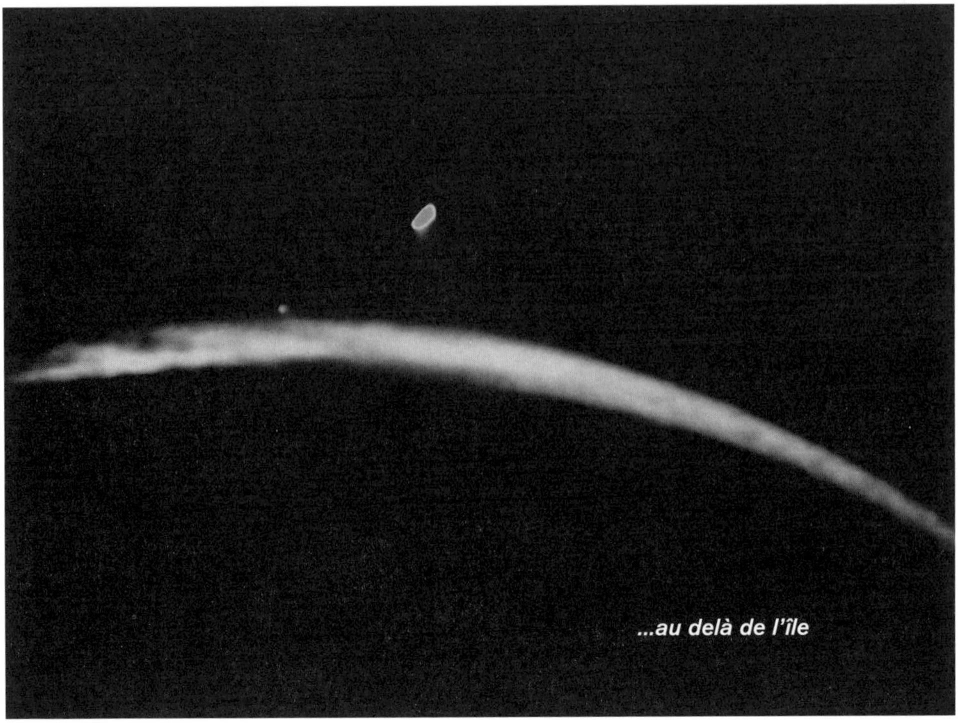

...au delà de l'île

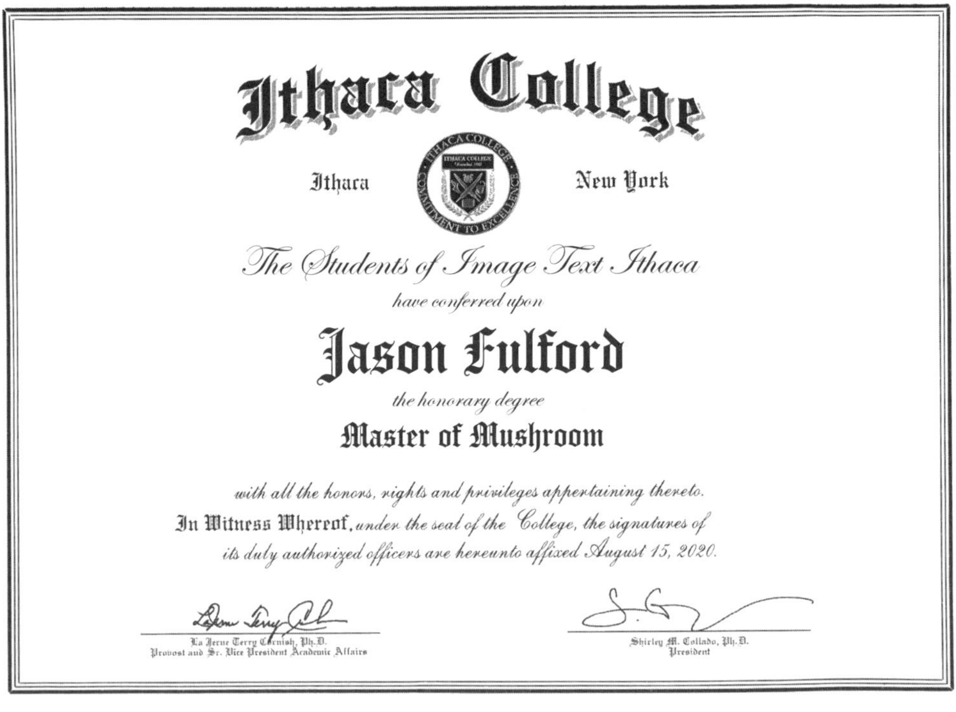

Ithaca College

Ithaca 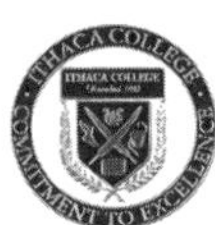 New York

The Students of Image Text Ithaca

have conferred upon

Jason Fulford

the honorary degree

Master of Mushroom

with all the honors, rights and privileges appertaining thereto.

In Witness Whereof, *under the seal of the College, the signatures of its duly authorized officers are hereunto affixed August 15, 2020.*

La Jerne Terry Cornish, Ph.D.
Provost and Sr. Vice President Academic Affairs

Shirley M. Collado, Ph.D.
President

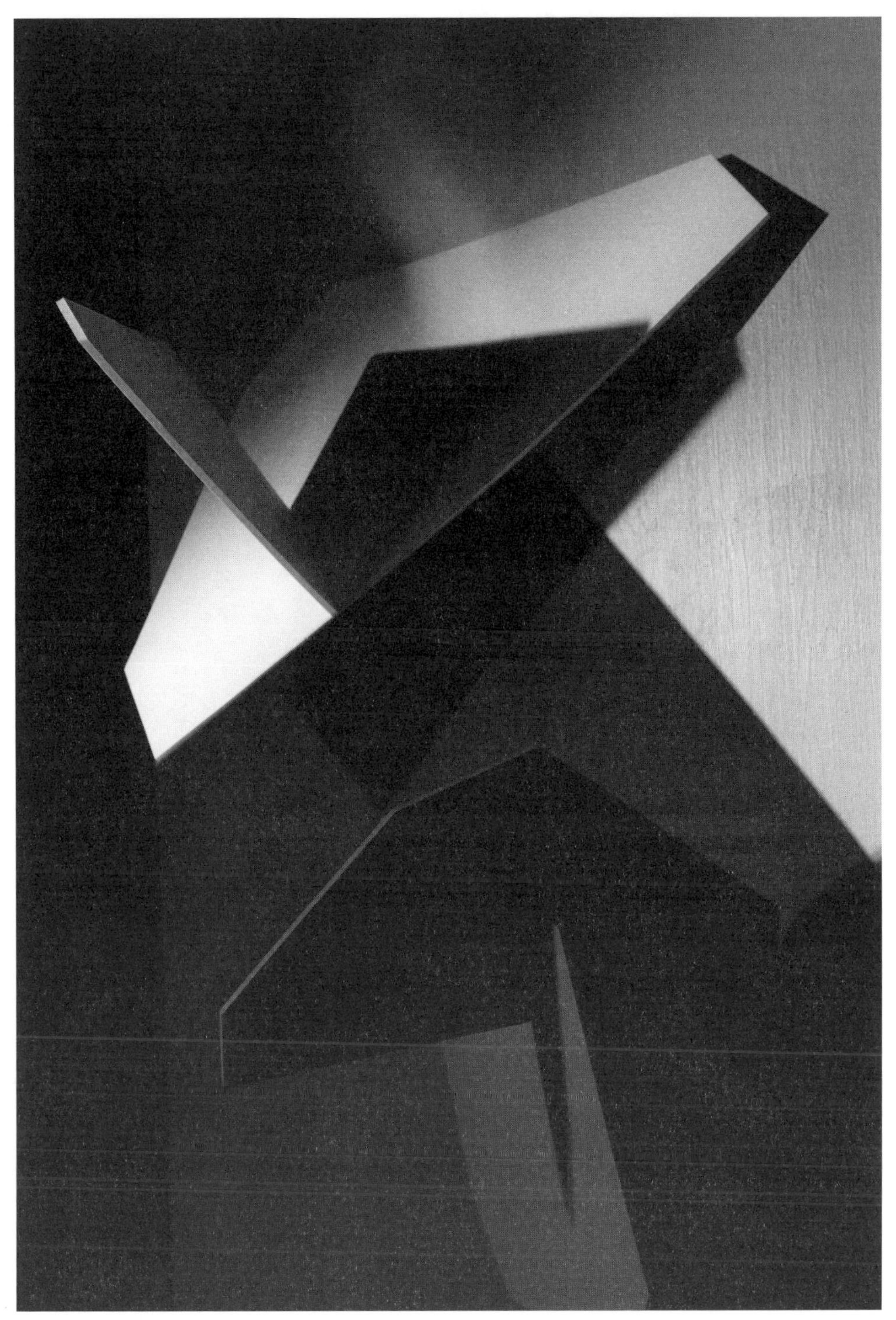

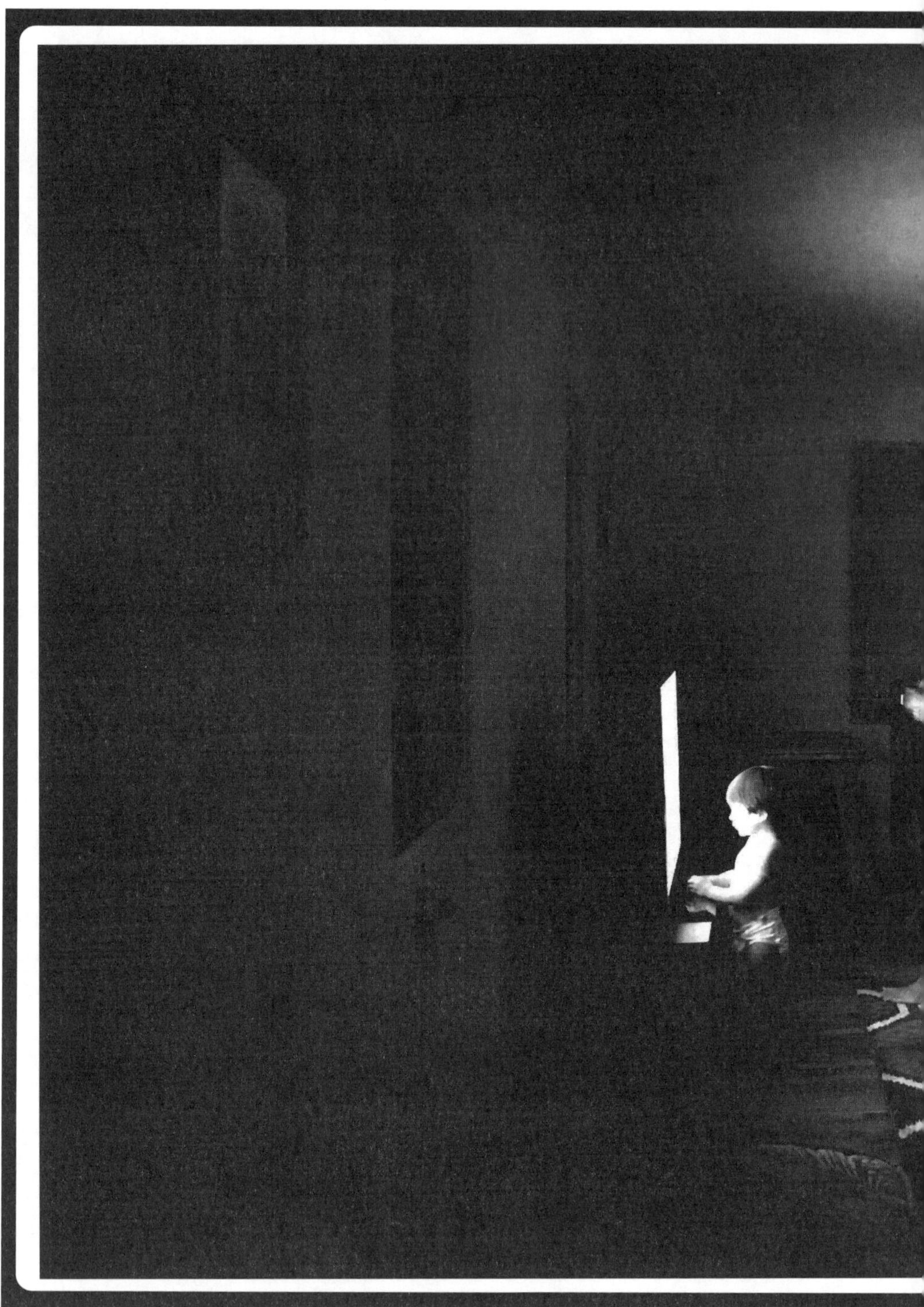

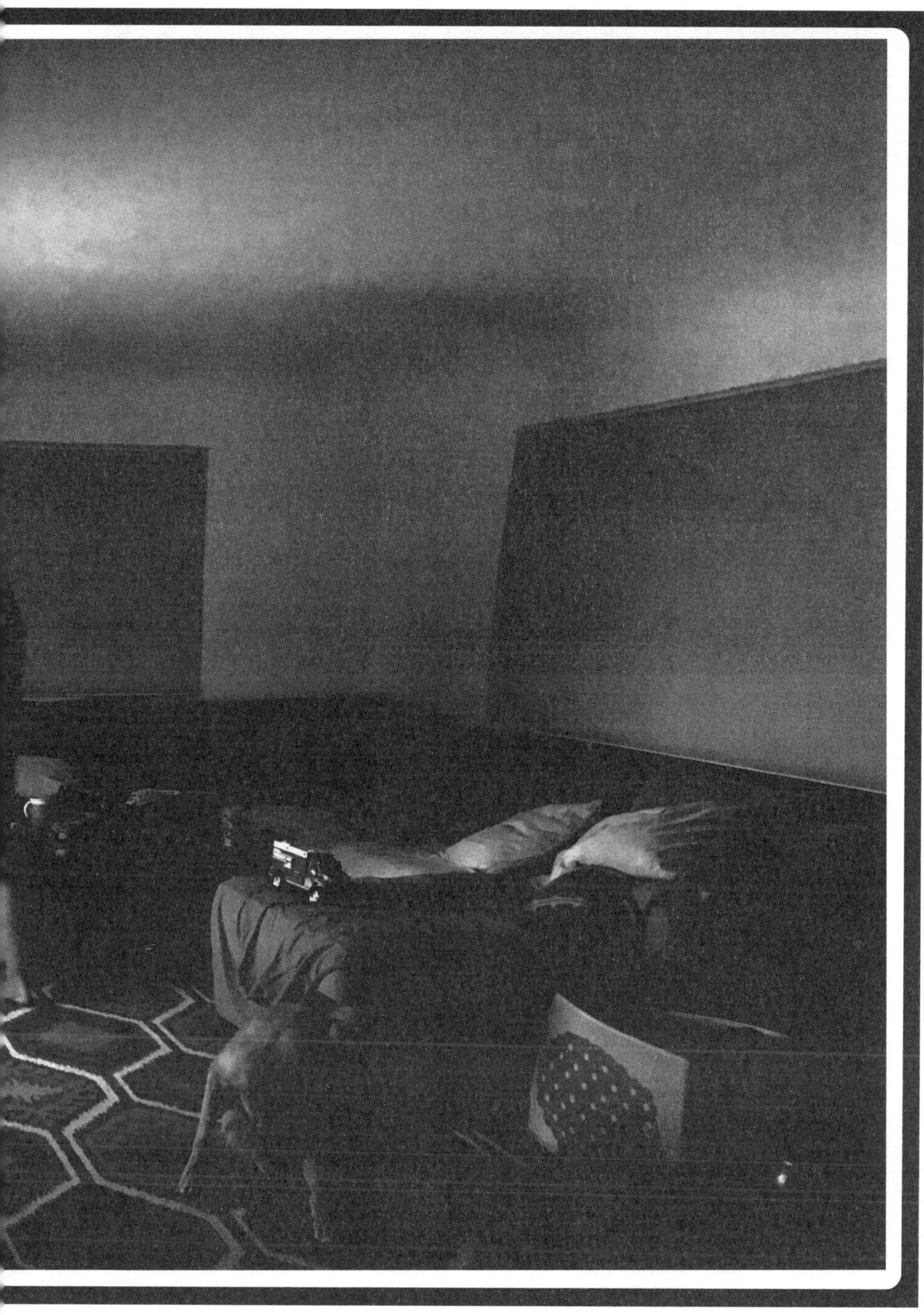

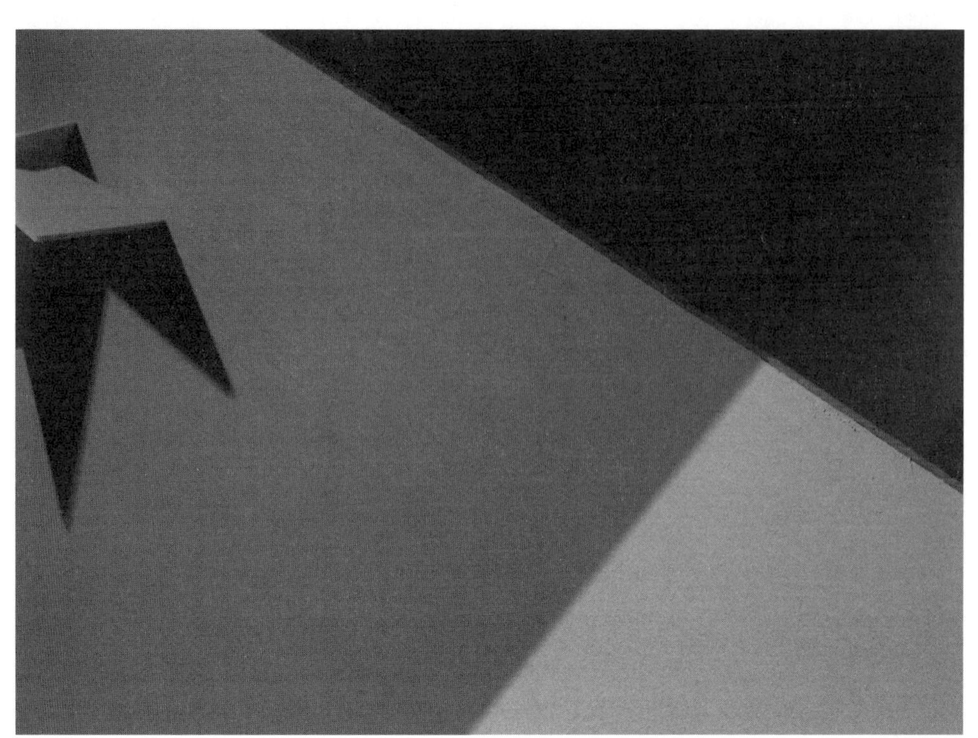

BURN
THE
COMMITTEE

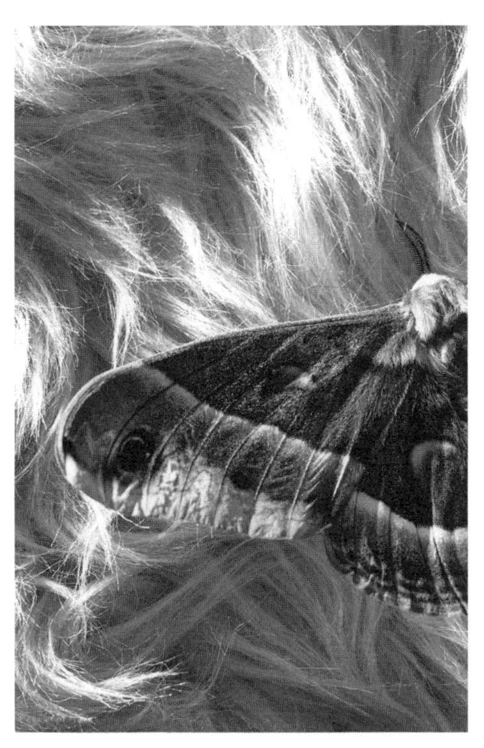

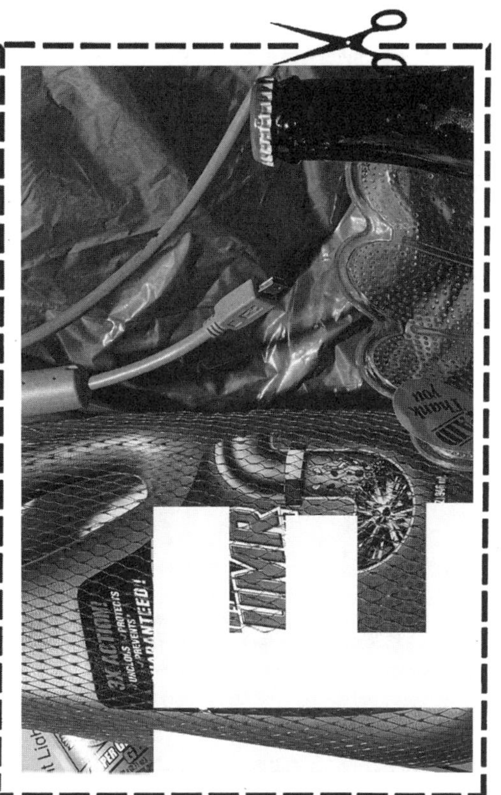
3X ACTION!
GUARANTEED!
Thank you

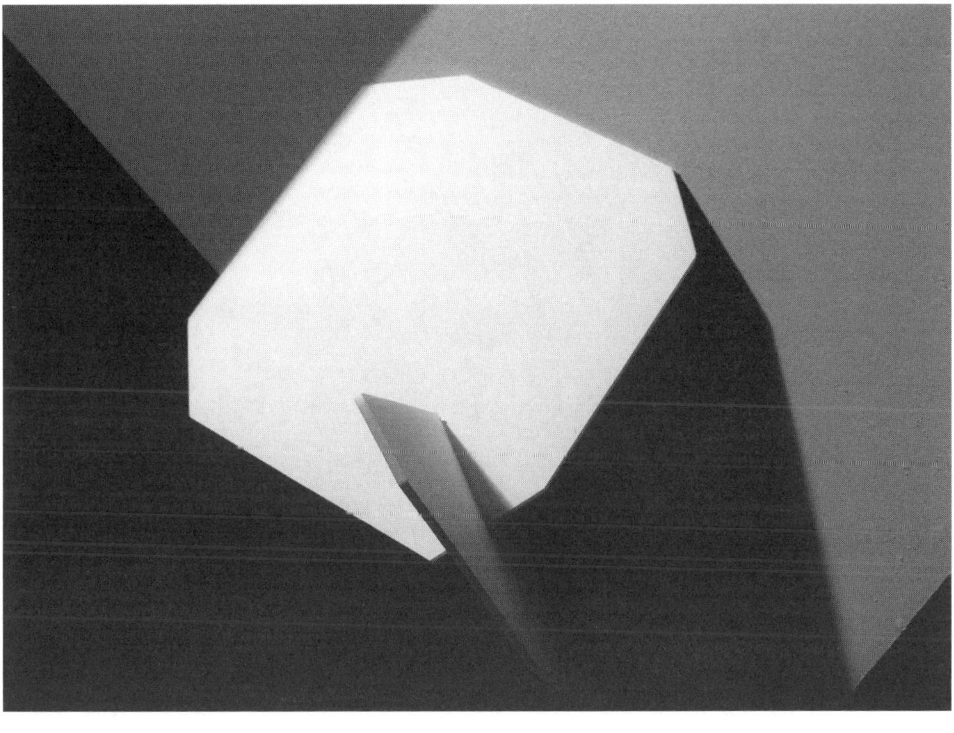

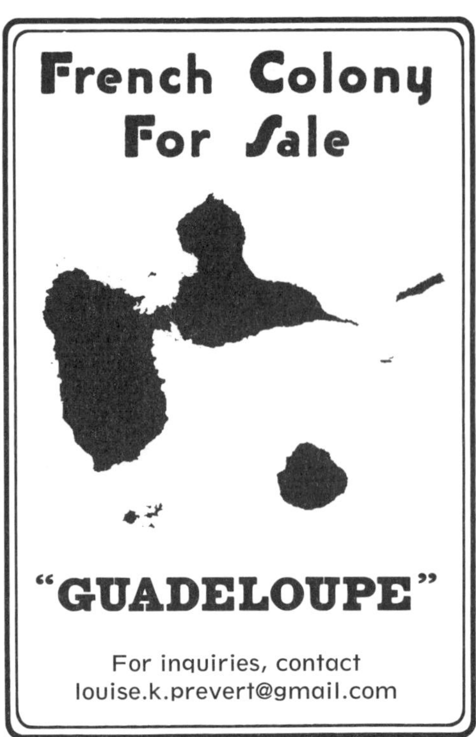
French Colony
For Sale
"GUADELOUPE"
For inquiries, contact
louise.k.prevert@gmail.com

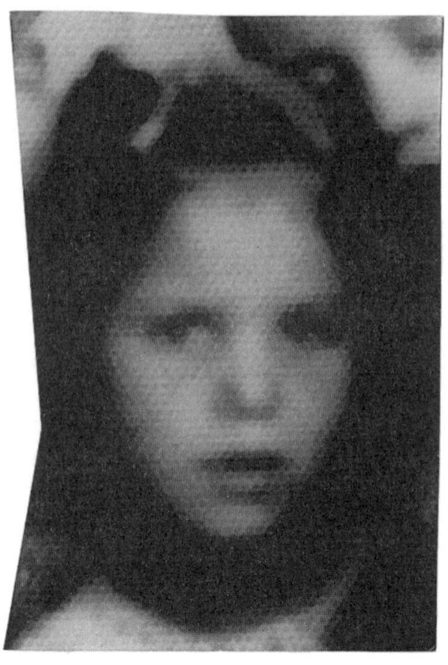

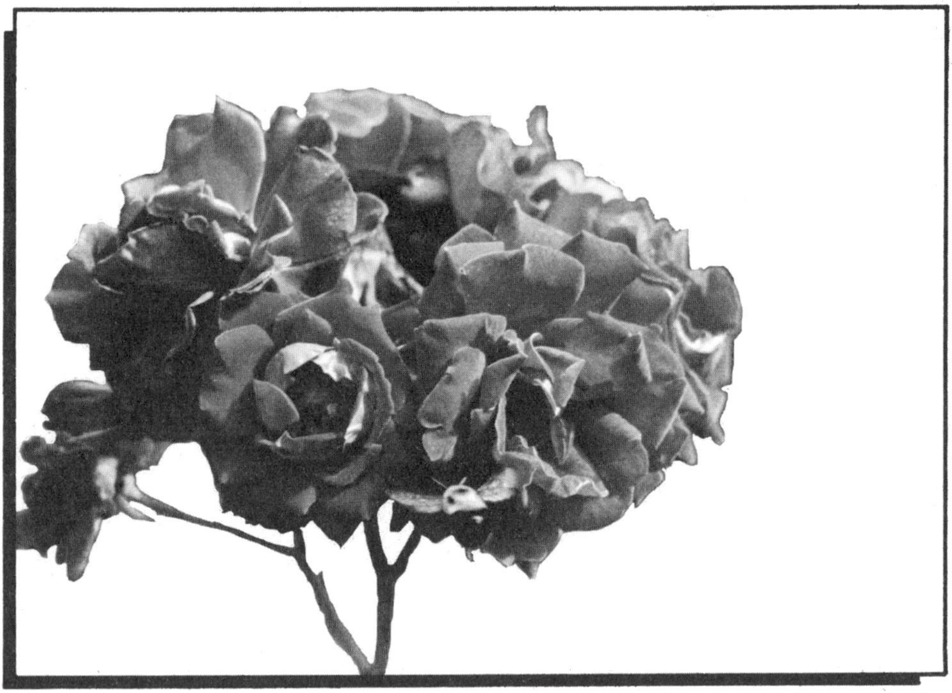

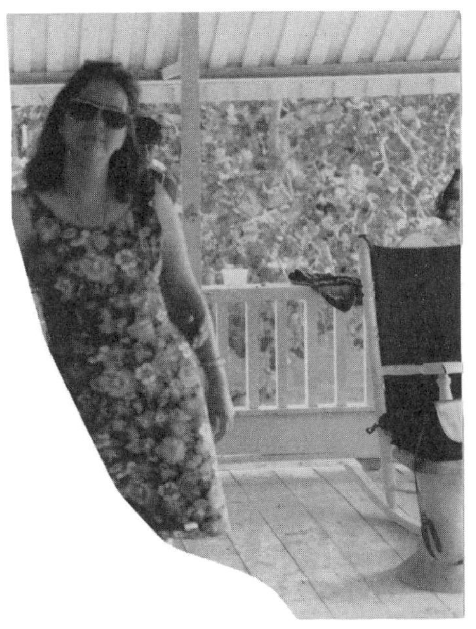

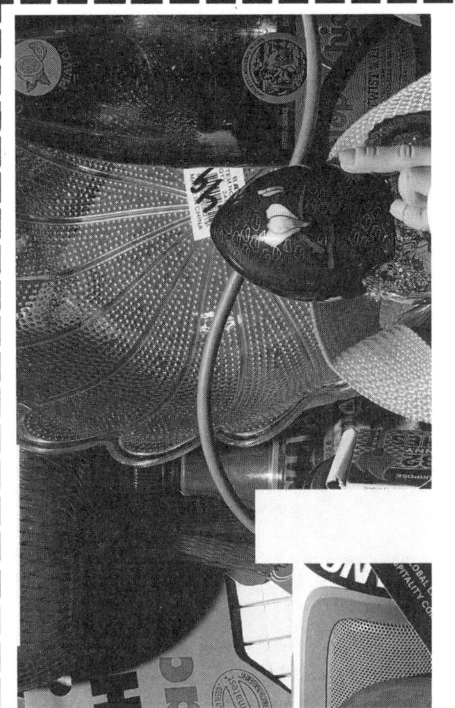

when my son was born that there really wasn't much for me to do. I essentially spent fourteen hours patting my wife's hand and repeating, "you're doing great..." A week before I dropped her off we had talked about me missing the birth, she assured me she'd be okay. "I know," I said, "but what if? What if you need me, what if she needs me?" I knew it was unlikely, I knew there was no possible situation where I'd be more useful then the doctors and nurses in the room but I didn't know what else to say. I felt like I was setting a precedent of absence and I worried that absence would affect my ability to bond with my daughter. I still think it might have.

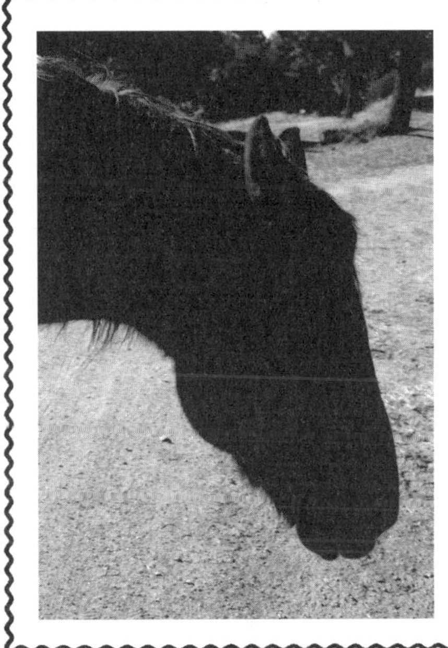

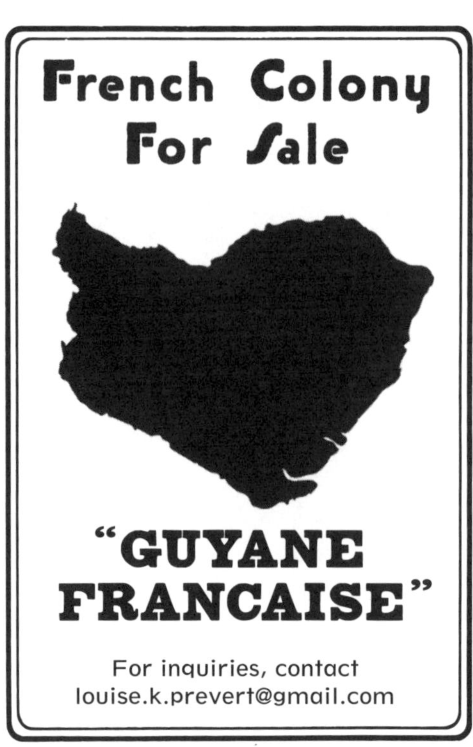
French Colony
For Sale
"GUYANE
FRANCAISE"
For inquiries, contact
louise.k.prevert@gmail.com

Will Photograph
objects for $$$
MP
FLOWCODE
PRIVACY.FLOWCODE.COM

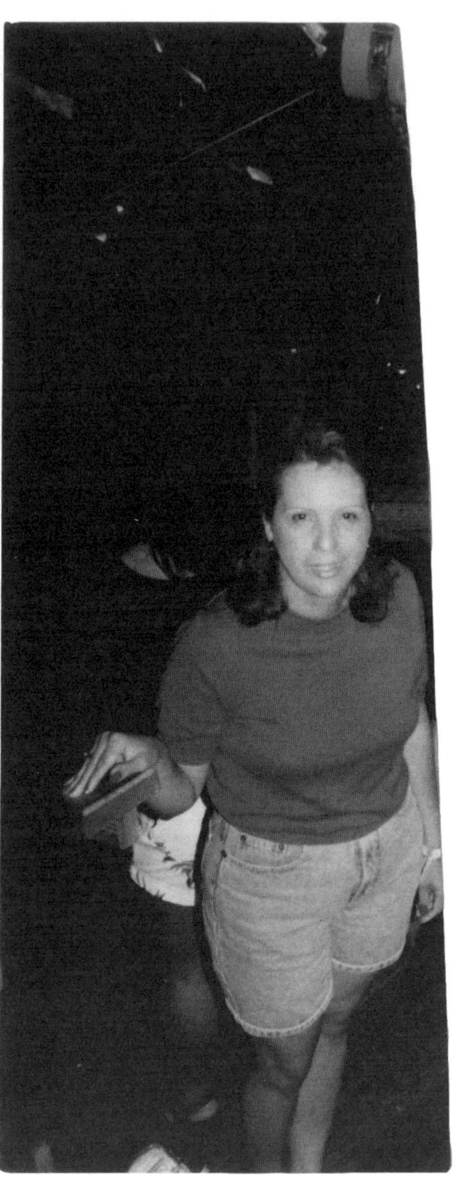

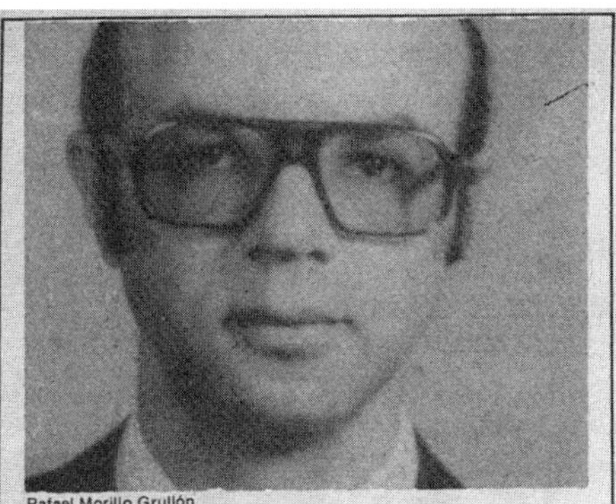

Rafael Morillo Grullón

Primera fila

Un mes después de haber desaparecido en las inmediaciones del pico Duarte, la gente pregunta con inquietud qué ha sido del ingeniero Rafael Morillo Grullón, cabeza de una estimada familia de Santiago. Nadie podría explicar racionalmente por qué, pero se siente en el ambiente la creencia de que el ingeniero Morillo Grullón está con vida en alguna parte de la geografía nacional, aunque probablemente muy extraviado. Su esposa, su madre, hijos, una hermana y otros familiares hicieron ayer una dramática exposición en el programa El Gordo de la Semana y dijeron sin lugar a equívoco que estaban seguros de que su pariente había sido localizado con vida y, que detalles de gran importancia estarían en disposición de ofrecerlos al presidente de la República. Todo cuanto contribuya a aclarar esta desaparición hay que hacerlo. La tranquilidad del país así lo demanda.

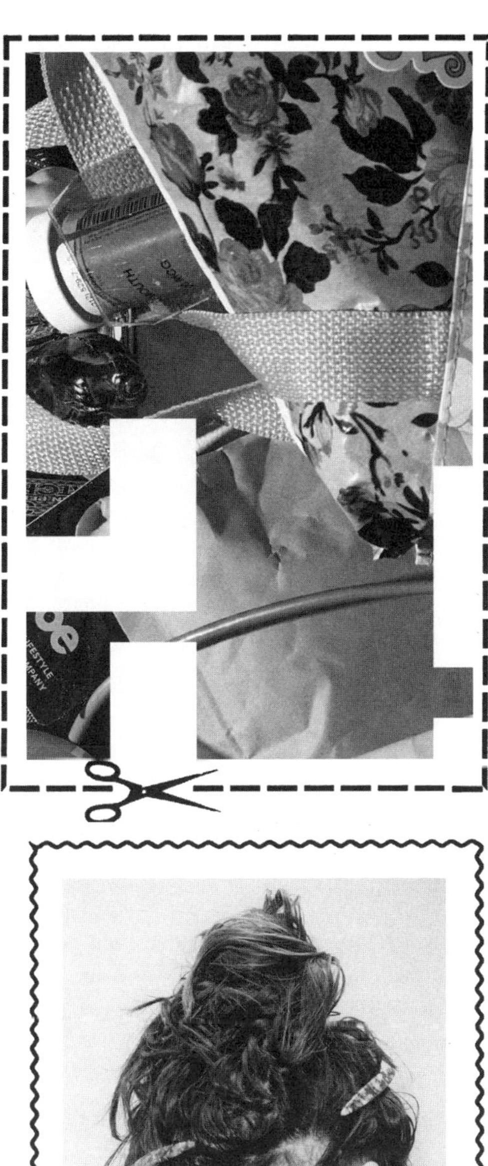

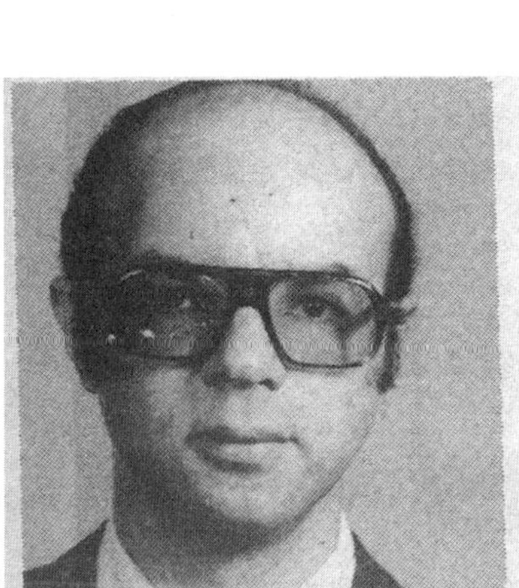

Rafael Morillo Grullón

Ingeniero Morillo

Organizaciones de izquierda reclaman de las autoridades esclarecer el caso del ingeniero Rafael Morillo Grullón, desaparecido mientras bajaba de una excursión del pico Duarte.

El Partido Comunista Dominicano, (PCD) de los Trabajadores Dominicanos (PTD), la Unión Patriótica Antiimperialista (UPA) y Militantes de de Izquierda Unida (IU), pidieron al presidente Balaguer ordenar investigar el caso.

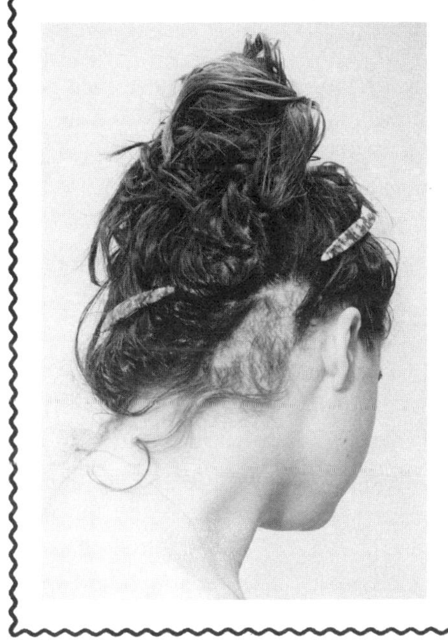

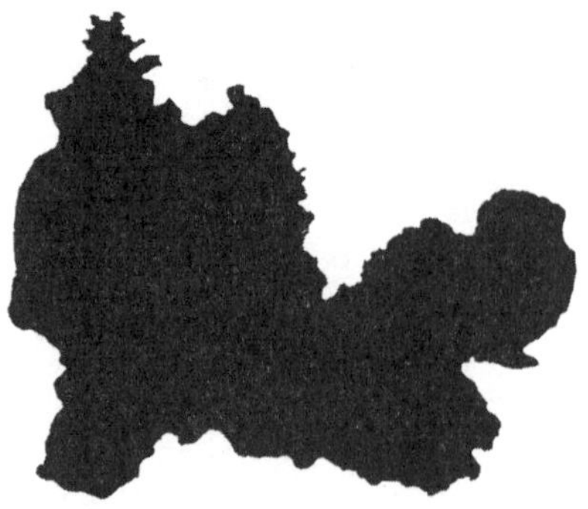

My wife was in labor for eleven hours before she finally got permission for me to enter the hospital. I was trying to put our son to bed but I was constantly on my phone and it distracted him. As he finally began to settle and curl into bed I told my wife I thought it would be ten or fifteen more minutes. She responded with two quick, successive texts, "Please come." "Come now."

I called my son's grandma up from downstairs and explained the situation. She outfitted herself in the same shroud of mask and gloves she had used through the airport and came up to stay with my son. He hadn't yet fallen asleep and was now re-energized by the burst of

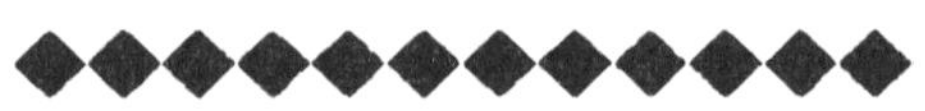

1919 on the bottle, when it was first made I guess, not the coaster but the liquor, the same year he came here and this box from New York traveled where he traveled, up 95, further north. The bottle of liquor in my fridge now, bottle of liquor on the table, though it could have been on his restaurant's bartop, too. I wonder if he poured spritzes, if he poured shots of Cynar or Frenet, but mostly, I wonder about the spritzes. I walk in Padova and see, it's 5pm, the flaming goblets in the hands of beautiful women, manicured hands delicately balancing thin cigarettes—they place their stemmed glasses down on rot-iron tables that balance on the bright cobblestone. But here I am with a cheap paper circle to tuck under my glass, I haven't actually done it yet. A cheap paper circle just to hold the base of a heavy thing in place.

My grandfather has stopped buying the paper daily, because it's not really local anymore and it's expensive, and instead does crosswords from a book my brother gave him. He shows me one of the harder puzzles, where you have to figure out where each answer goes and fill in the black squares too, which he has given up on, because it is too hard. And I show him how a crossword is laid out like a butterfly, how if you fold it in the middle it will match the other half in structure. He looks at me like I have made his life new. *Caitlin*, he says. He cannot believe it. He has been doing a crossword every day for my whole life. There is a crossword dictionary whose pages are dirty from use. He had no idea.

I teach him how to propagate a plant too, how to cut the pilea as close to the dirt as possible and then stick it in water. I sacrifice the tie from my hair to keep the paper towel in place, and on the drive back it is blowing all around me in the wind.

French Colony For Sale

"LA REUNION"

For inquiries, contact
louise.k.prevert@gmail.com

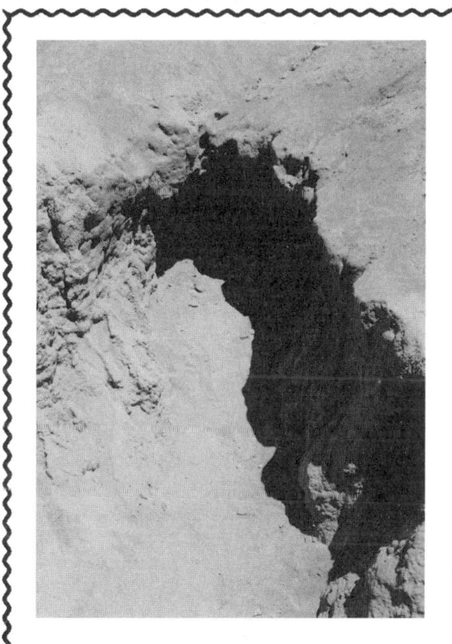

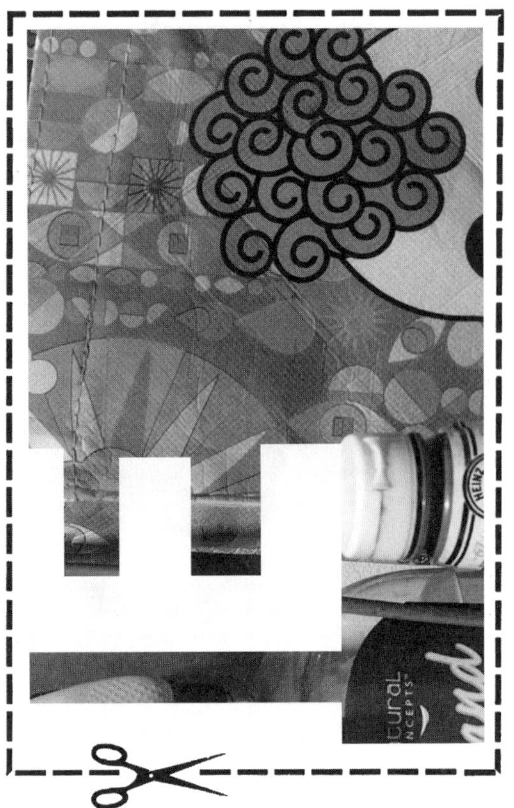

CUP OF CUM

Tibor, a middle-aged man, with day-old facial hair, thin silver-rimmed glasses, and a completely forgettable face, sat at his desk in a lab coat. Behind him like a wall of soldiers were no less than 6 students, all young and eager. They stared at me, as he finished with the keys on his keyboard. He pressed the last key with a marked action, signifying that he had completed his task, and turned his shoulders to me, his eyes still on the screen, his hands paused above the keyboard. You have cancer. His tone was flat with each word democratically delivered. I nodded once,

(*continued on page 68*)

INCOMPLETE LIST OF HINGES

BOOKS
DOORS
FORGOTTEN
OBJECTS
HANDS
MIRRORS
PAGES
PARKING LOTS
PLANETS
PLANTS
SHORES
SIDEWALKS
STARS
STREETS
TELEPHONES
WEATHER
WINDOWS
WORDS
ADD YOUR OWN:

Is the house on fire or is it underwater? It doesn't matter; it's untenable. The antibiotic I'm taking, it makes all of the nerves in my hands leap to the surface, so that each time I take a shower it feels like the water is burning them, and I turn up my palms and wiggle my fingers. The pain in my back has shifted upward into spasms around my shoulder blades. I am acutely aware of the tendons around my knees, at the bottoms of my thighs, and how once I had a boyfriend who offered to hold my camera for me if I ever lost use of my hands. He seemed less concerned with my hands and more concerned that I could still make photographs of him. The antibiotic is a big pill that I can't take with dairy. The antibiotic makes me fussy and sleepy and subdued.

The way the doctor looks at me as she scans the list, trying to soothe my body. I have forgotten about the lump, which happened less than a month ago; already I have new concerns, new medical maladies. Already my body is churning. Already I am wrong wrong the things within my body are wrong wrong and I am late late and she looks at me with disgust. The world outside of the window, the people who live on 58th Street, they look out their windows with disgust too.

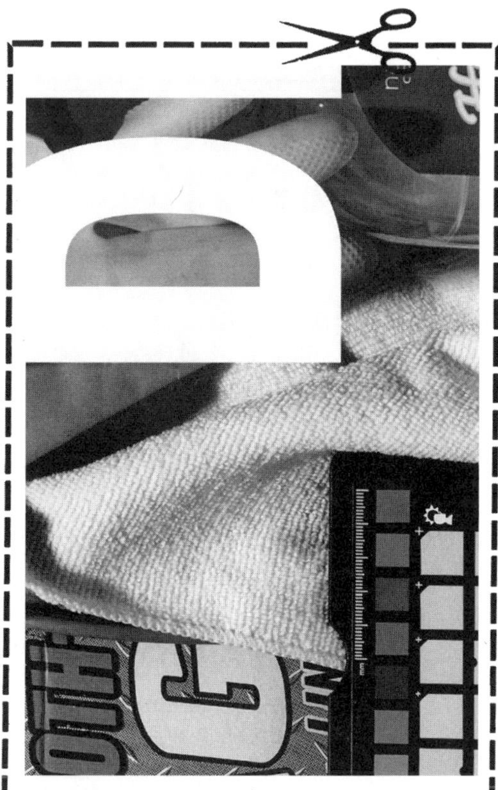

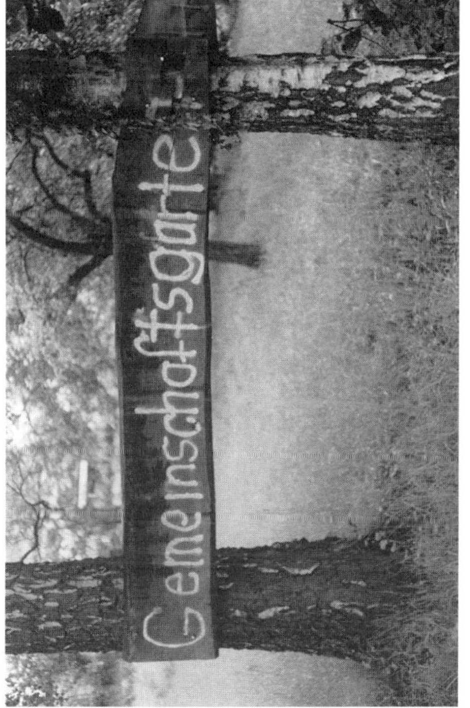

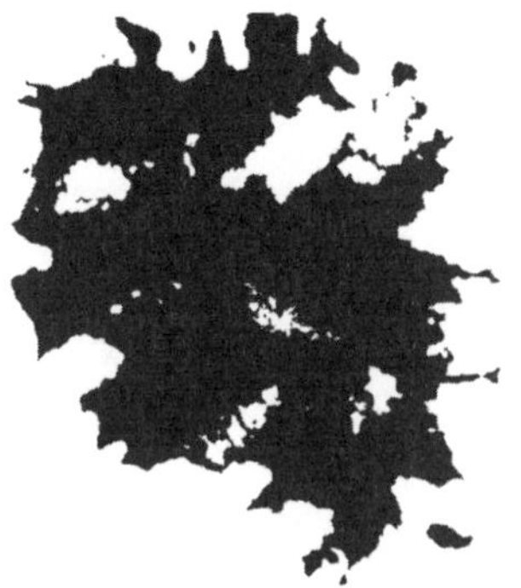

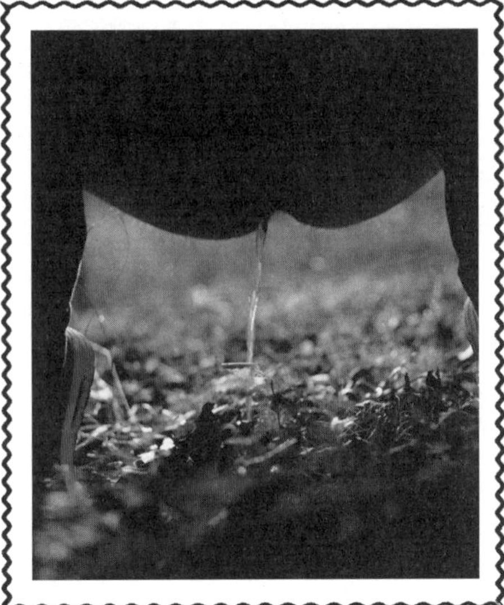

activity. Grandma set about a frustrating, hands-off, socially-distanced form of babysitting that mostly involved following my son from room to room while he ran about lawlessly. I found out later that he finally put himself to bed about an hour and a half later.

I drove to the hospital as quickly as I could and pulled on my own face mask as I sprinted through the parking lot. The late hour meant that the hospital was quiet and some of the additional safety protocols were relaxed a bit. The clerk recognized me when she saw me running through the parking lot and she helped expedite my entry into the hospital and escorted me upstairs to the delivery suite. When she knocked on the door I could hear my daughter already crying inside and I knew I hadn't made it in time. After a quick exchange of names and a squirt of hand sanitizer I was allowed into the room and the attending nurse told me I was only two minutes late. The official time of birth was 9:07, the clock said 9:09. They told me my daughter was born with her own hand resting on her cheek, I didn't see it.

My son has a picture board book with a banal story about a boy who helps his mother with the daily chores. It's meant to help him learn household vocabulary. They go to the park and to the grocery store, they meet friends, chat and wave and touch. They pick out fruit and milk and bread. They return home for lunch

Shirley you must be kidding

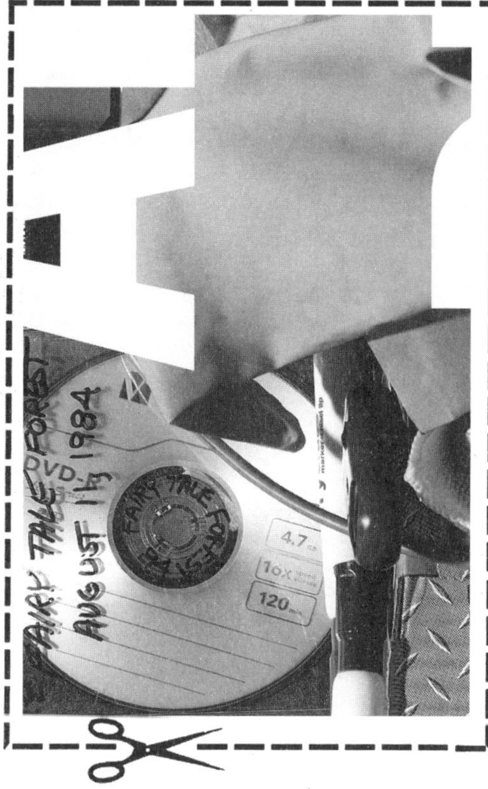

Send me a letter w/ your return address about an experience you've had pissing, and I will send you back pictures of me pissing, bound with staples in a zine.*

PO BOX 34582
SAN DIEGO, CA
USA 92163

* If you do not send a letter you will have to pay $10 for it.

With the same resoluteness sh… ago … of thi… cts her … ph whe… ne-one … rail of is… es, whic… nd-sca… ev-ery … She era… in-timate dance. The delicate act of combing through a heap of ashes.

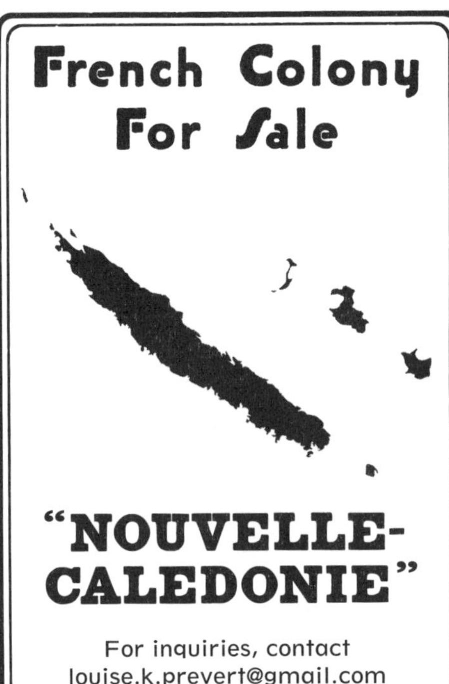

SEARCHING FOR:

S K E M J Q E M Q K F M I Y T
K U F G F E H E G Y R D L T C
Y M P E H W O G E O U N L I O
N O F E G M K Y F B E X U R P
P E J X R E M S Z I D D S A I
V I D P H I N X G Z Z P I L P
N B R P Z A M H T R P Q O U W
R S E B R Q B P S W O U N S K
K M H T P O C Z O M H Z R N X
V O T Q R Z K V C S R N X I L
C L O S E N O M I L E Y X T E
J O M R X Y B O D Y D B H T W
F Z K J V O Y L X N N U Y B B
C R Q M Z Y T A A N N O Y K G
G Q E N Z U E G S X R P N V S

- MOTHER
- TRANSFORM
- BODY
- SUPERIMPOSE
- ILLUSION
- NEIGHBORS
- LIMONE
- JOY
- INSULARITY

o, mami carved herself out
s family picture. She extra
self out of every photogra
re she appears with son
else, leaving behind a t
olated, rectangular shap
h I now arrange into la
pes where she becomes
building in the skyline. S
ises and I reconstruct, our

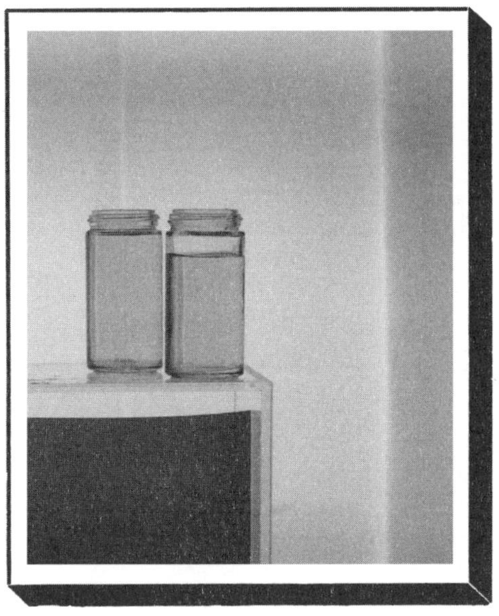

French Colony For Sale

"TAHITI"

For inquiries, contact
louise.k.prevert@gmail.com

Ithaca College

Ithaca

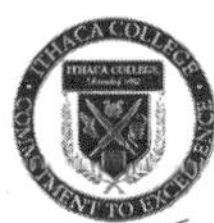

New York

The Trustees of Ithaca College,
upon the recommendation of the Faculty have conferred upon

Caitlín Anne Borruso

the degree

Master of Fine Arts

with all the honors, rights and privileges appertaining thereto.
In Witness Whereof, *under the seal of the College, the signatures of its duly authorized officers are hereunto affixed August 15, 2020.*

La Jerne Terry Cornish, Ph.D.
Provost and Sr. Vice President Academic Affairs

Shirley M. Collado, Ph.D.
President

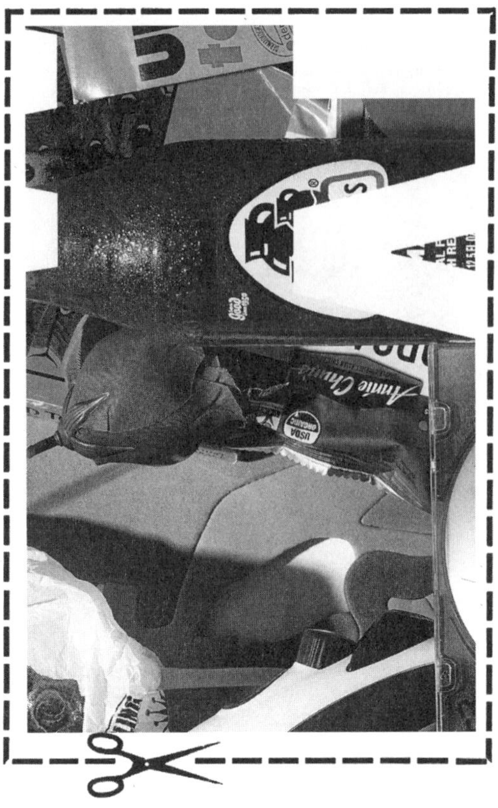

faire entendre
leurs voix
ma voix

se retrouver à travers elles

s'ancrer à leurs histoires

(*continued from page 62*)

the way men do when they make eye contact on the street. Tibor continued to specify the type of leukemia, and that I had a 30% chance of perishing, but he delivered that with the affirmative 70%. He asked me if I had banked my sperm, but in such a way that presumed, I had. Four minutes into having cancer and I'm making mistakes. He scribbled down a number on a yellow post-it note. It's 4:45, he said, They close at 5.

I arrived at the upper east side brownstone 7 minutes late. I'm handed 30 pages of documents to fill out. On the third page "your death" appears next to two checkboxes, a binary solution to my semen in the event of my certain death. It's the first time I would consider this question seriously. I checked "incinerate" and they hand me a small semi-translucent cup about the size of a side of macaroni salad and show me to a room.

The room had awkward proportions and was large for what it was, a room to masturbate in. The walls were a deep and uncomfortable red. It was dark, with just a single low wattage lamp casting a yellow light on the objects within the space. In the center of the room, across from a cheap 65" flat-screen TV and white Ikea bookshelf was a black padded Z-shaped

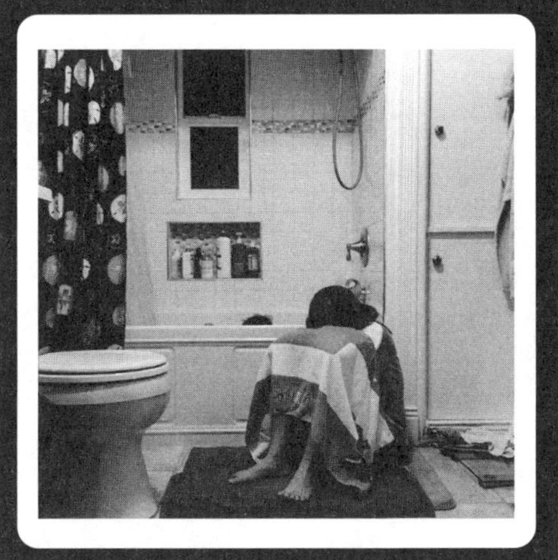

vinyl lounge chair. It was the same one I saw in a porno I stole from my father's collection as a kid. On the floor, just behind the chair, was a roll of that sterile and noisy white paper that doctors put over things in rooms like this, to give you the impression that this thin white barrier keeps you off the chair, just as it kept the hundreds of men jerking themselves off before you.

I approached the bookshelf, which in this situation contained no books, but instead a library of pornographic material. There were dozens of half-stained magazines, and hundreds of DVDs, some store-bought, many homemade.

(*continued on page 74*)

and laundry and they check the mail. They share a friendly greeting with their mailman. 'Hello mailman Pete.' My son has already outgrown this book, he's mastered 'apple' and 'milk' and 'sock' months ago and his new favorite book is about dinosaurs. I still haven't mastered 'pachycephalosaurus.' My son still calls every postal worker 'Pete' everyday though. Since the quarantine, we don't take him to the park or the grocery store anymore so Pete has become his sole social activity beyond our living room. He rushes to the window every time he hears the postal truck and he shouts 'hi Pete, hi Pete.' Pete never hears him or maybe he just doesn't know he's named Pete. It doesn't discourage my son at all. Our local postal service is,

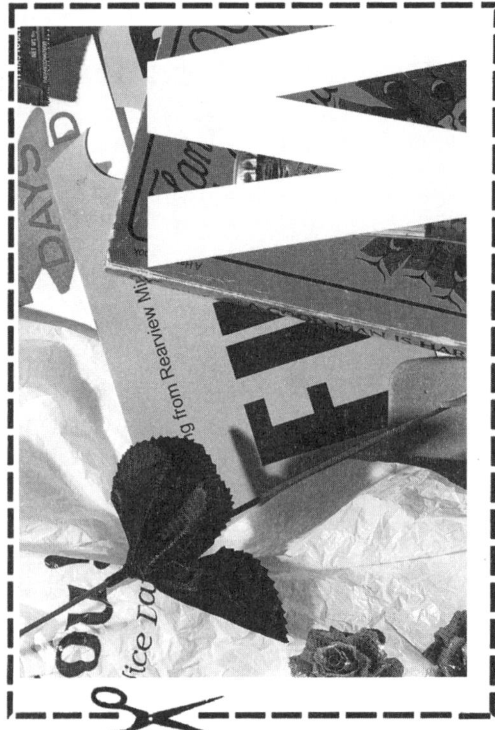

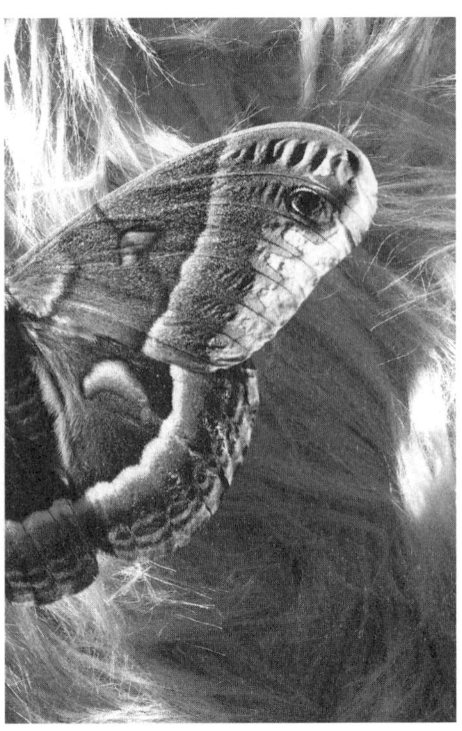

Ithaca College

Ithaca

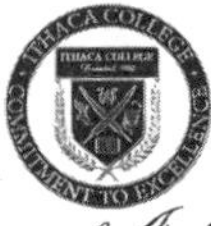

New York

The Trustees of Ithaca College,

upon the recommendation of the Faculty have conferred upon

Irit Reinheimer

the degree

Master of Fine Arts

with all the honors, rights and privileges appertaining thereto.

In Witness Whereof, *under the seal of the College, the signatures of its duly authorized officers are hereunto affixed August 15, 2020.*

La Jerne Terry Cornish, Ph.D.
Provost and Sr. Vice President Academic Affairs

Shirley M. Collado, Ph.D.
President

When my father disappeared, my grandfather paid Balaguer a visit to the presidential palace. He was allowed in only because, as young boys, they had gone to school together in the city of Navarrete, the memories of those days softening the president into hearing him out.

"I came to ask you for my son's body." Please. I promise not to retaliate; I just want to see his body and say goodbye."

As they spoke, I imagine their eyes watering, their glasses a temporal wall to conceal their distrust of each other. I picture them as boys, bright beyond the confines of their small town, eating mangoes on the side of the road, the trails of juice drying on their arms as they watched the cars speed by on the big road that leads to the sea in Puerto Plata. Two boys who would end up on opposite sides of their island's history.

That day, my grandfather walked out of the palace without answers and with a promise of a thorough investigation on the disappearance, a promise both men knew was a lie. In the missing person photo they used in the newspapers, my father was wearing thick-rimmed glasses, the same kind he sported in his college graduation photograph.

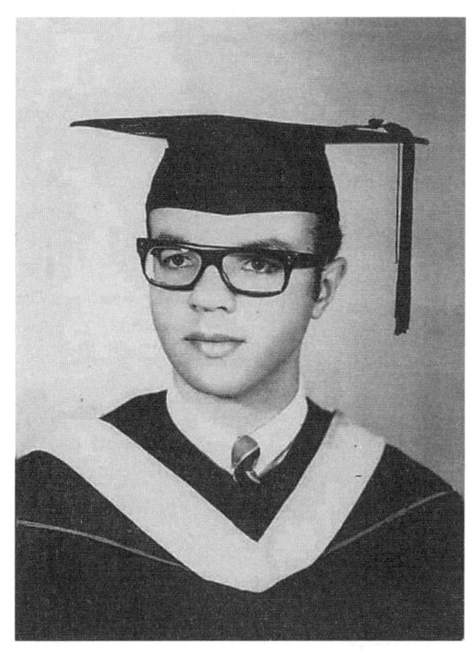

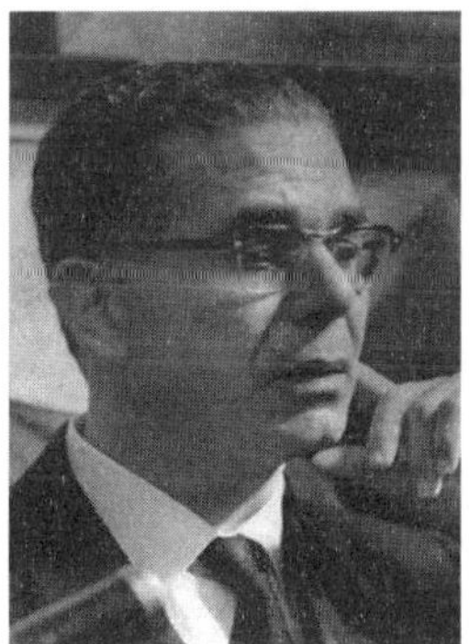

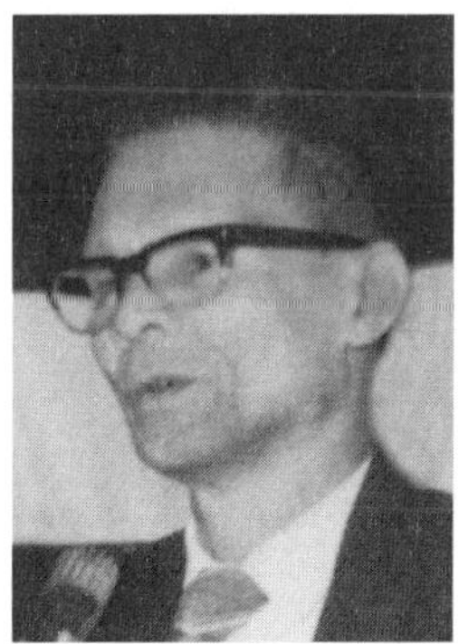

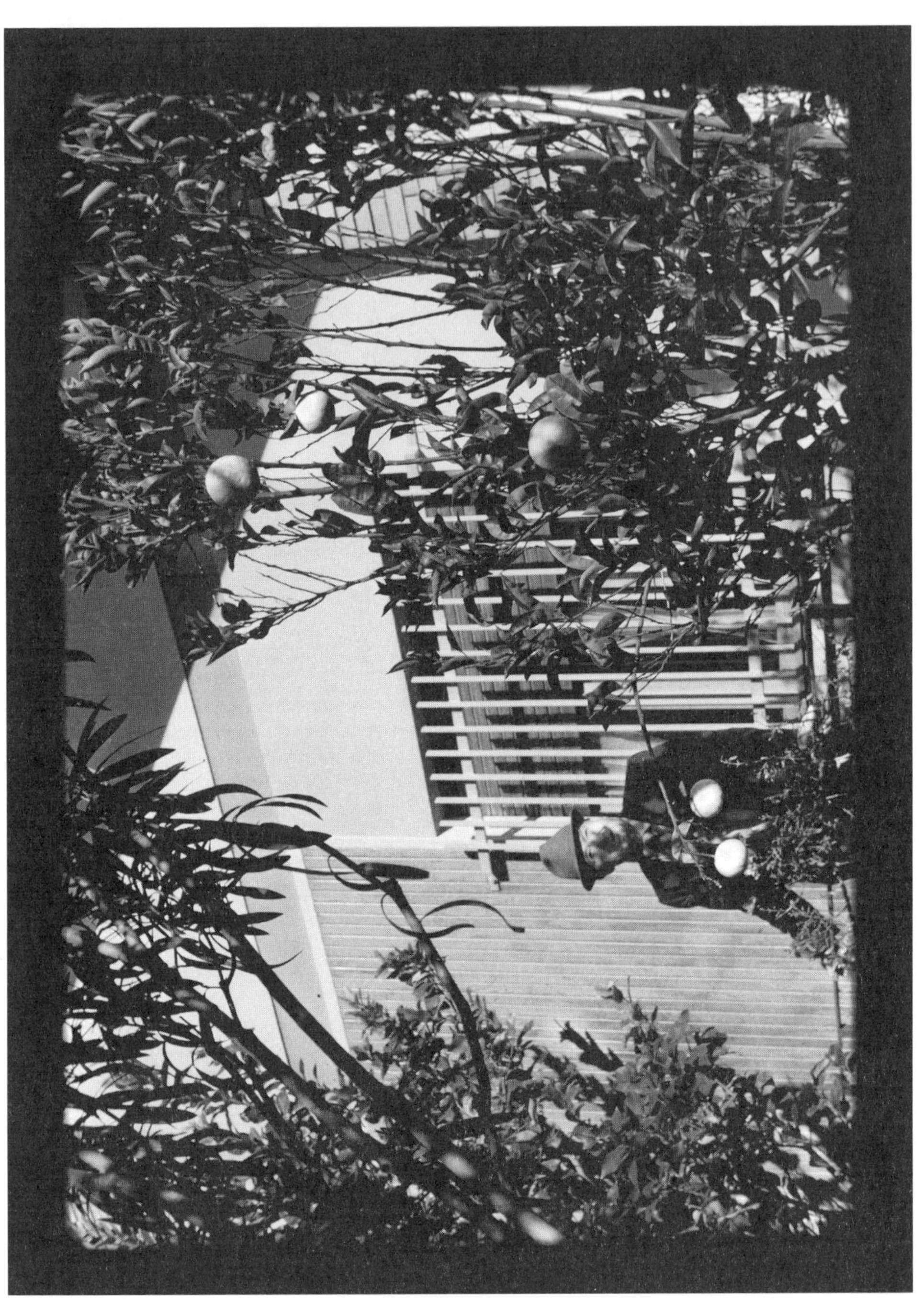

citrus

other relevant words

plantain tree ash tree strawberry guava lime hydrate gold rush cultivated crab apple papaia calcium oxide segment godsend punk algarroba bean fanny division stinker tail maharaja gang common fig tree behind corn whsikey ruby-red surgical incision birdlime crew figure tooshie lounge about caustic li lime yield true guava edible corn crummy burnt lime tramp rear incision locust pod chintzy bay laurel linden mandarin crimson intellectual nourishment orange river corn whisky fundament hobo tush sponge alder tree waste one,s time discussion section gravy bunch up cluster common elder layabout loafer crabapple hindquarters part leechee idler fluxing lime calcium hydrate scum bag monkey-bread tree bundle cherry red red cherry-red backside hydrated lime rat carob tree clump loll around solid food calcium hydroxide carmine sweet almond chocolate tree blood-red cadge melon tree tail end seat orangeness orangish sleazy quest loll butt ruby balsa wood quicklime plane section basswoodn fuck off manna from heaven cheesy clustering mooch grub so-and-so calx reddish frig around papaya tree true laurel bunch together tinny nutrient arse posterior teakwood stone fruit hind end common fig buns can mulberry tree puke stinkpot boom department bonanza cerise tamarindo lowlife scarlet wild apple ruddy ugli ugly clavus dirty dog skunk linden tree cheap clementine tree lotyellow yellow river lemon

(*continued from page 69*)

Along the top of the bookshelf, scattered among the matter, were square tissue boxes with subtle paisley patterns on them, a tissue trapped in the plastic mouth waited to be grabbed to wipe the cum off your dick or the tears from your eyes. Next to the tissues and on the floor were Purell bottles so you could cleanse your hands of the reproductive material that the tissues missed. The room smelled sour, like semen that's been exposed to air for too long, and sterile with alcohol. I stood there for a few minutes in silence taking in the room, my situation, and listening to the secretary just outside the door typing.

I reached for my phone, turned the volume off, and went to two-lips.com. What ended up in that ¼-lb salad cup, given the opportunity, could only create the saddest child in the world. After adding my own tissue to the pile, I scrubbed my hands with the alcohol, exited into the shaming brightness of the hall, and rang the service bell. I was finished. I signed the receipt for $860, a three-year contract.

Ithaca College

Ithaca

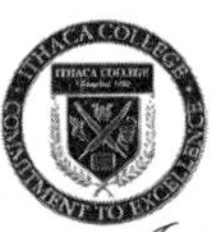

New York

The Trustees of Ithaca College,

upon the recommendation of the Faculty have conferred upon

Cable Hoover

the degree

Master of Fine Arts

with all the honors, rights and privileges appertaining thereto.

In Witness Whereof, *under the seal of the College, the signatures of its duly authorized officers are hereunto affixed August 15, 2020.*

La Jerne Terry Cornish, Ph.D.
Provost and Sr. Vice President Academic Affairs

Shirley M. Collado, Ph.D.
President

The rose bush blooms in the last few days of February, yellow, a softer yellow than I imagined. When I was picking it out in the garden center at Lowe's, it was warm and there were bees and I couldn't see any of the tags properly for fear of the thorns. I step outside every day to look at it, just to make sure it's still alive. Yesterday it rained and the rose bush is still spattered with water, the milkweed is happy, I have not been watering it enough and it wilted a little. I crouch to try and weed — I don't know what is good plant and bad plant — and there are tiny sprigs next to the basil and I pinch one between my fingers and pull aside the mask to sniff it and the tiny sprigs are also basil, it's all basil and mint. I leave them be. On Sunday night we hear someone outside cooing at the outdoor cat and so I go outside to assure them that she has an owner, I don't know her name but she has a flea collar on today which is an upgrade from last week. Anna comes out and tells us that the cat lives, sometimes, in the house that used to have a pet pig. Before your time, she explains to me. The neighbor and her two daughters look at the cat and decide she is too young; they each pet her and then they make their way home. Anna offers me rosemary. Our tiny side yard is where all of my socializing happens, with neighbors who walk by and see me crouching; I have always loved a squat.

a hum
reverberates
both *with*
and from
the body

nommer
pointer
lever
le voile
de la honte
du passé

dire leur noms
fort
mais sans crier

répéter sans cesse leurs noms
ne pas oublier leurs histoires

(*continued from page 15*)

past the apartheid wall. At meals, I'll be aware of the absence of conversations about the continuing forced displacements, the stealing of homes in East Jerusalem, the military detention of children, the rolling blackouts in Gaza. As I drink coffee in my cousin's living room, a half-hour away from it all, no one will speak of it. I have learned to be hyper-aware of the denial, what is not being said, what they refuse to see: the evidence of Palestinian life and land. As we sit together talking, I will remind myself of this other reality and it will keep me from being fully there.

On the phone, I notice her dementia impacting our conversations. She can't always remember what happened earlier in the day. She forgets the name of the person she saw over the weekend and expresses confusion about what month it is or what holiday just passed. It's not all the time, but often enough. It makes for frustrating conversations; I assure her it's okay that she can't remember. My memory is not so good, she repeats in every conversation. I ask her how that makes her feel. She often changes the subject.

My mother's memory was never sharp, and she would clip every article on memory loss she would happen upon. I know this because when I would visit her, I'd find these articles stacked by the sofa between bills and junk mail. There were articles held up by magnets on the fridge and shoved in the drawer of her nightstand. In her office, she had taped the articles to the articulated fluorescent desk lamp, along with a note to remind her of my partner's pronouns. The lamp flickered when it was turned on. The prospect of not remembering has frightened her for as long as I remember, but she won't talk to me about it.

I already miss her.

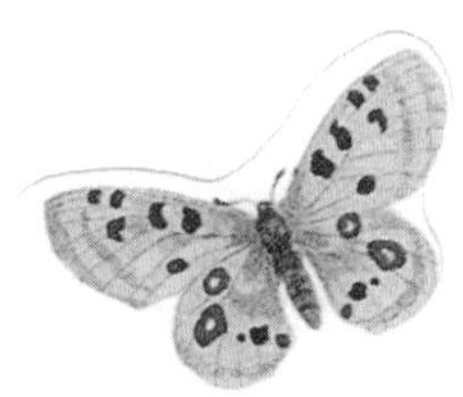

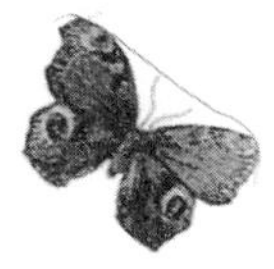

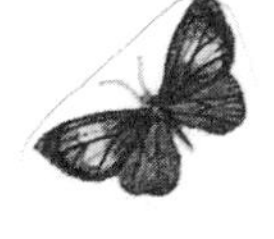

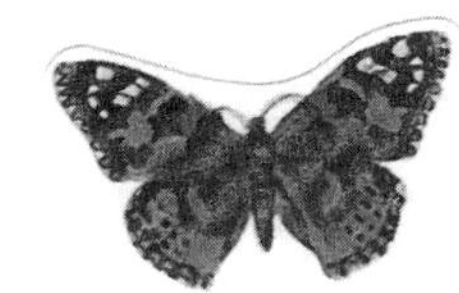

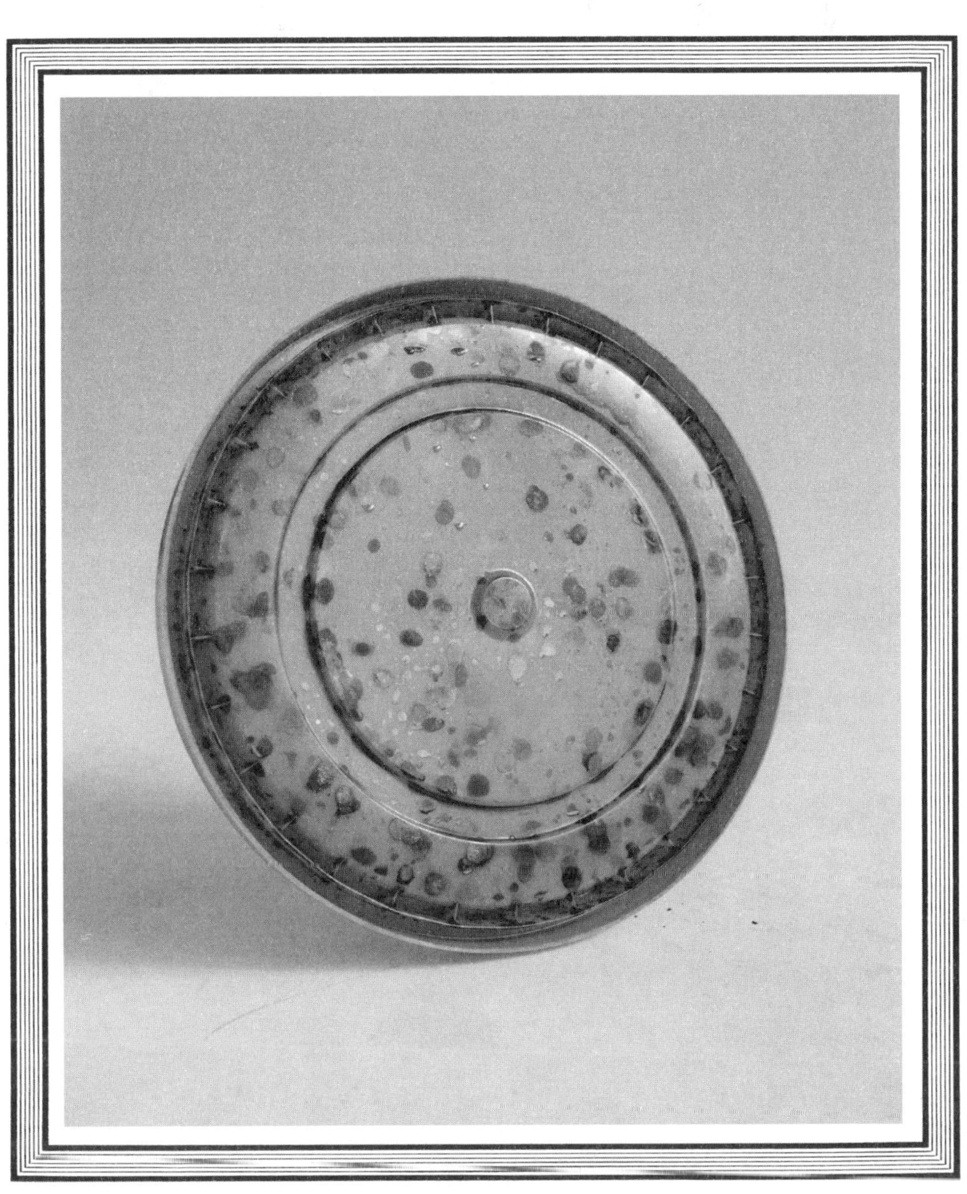

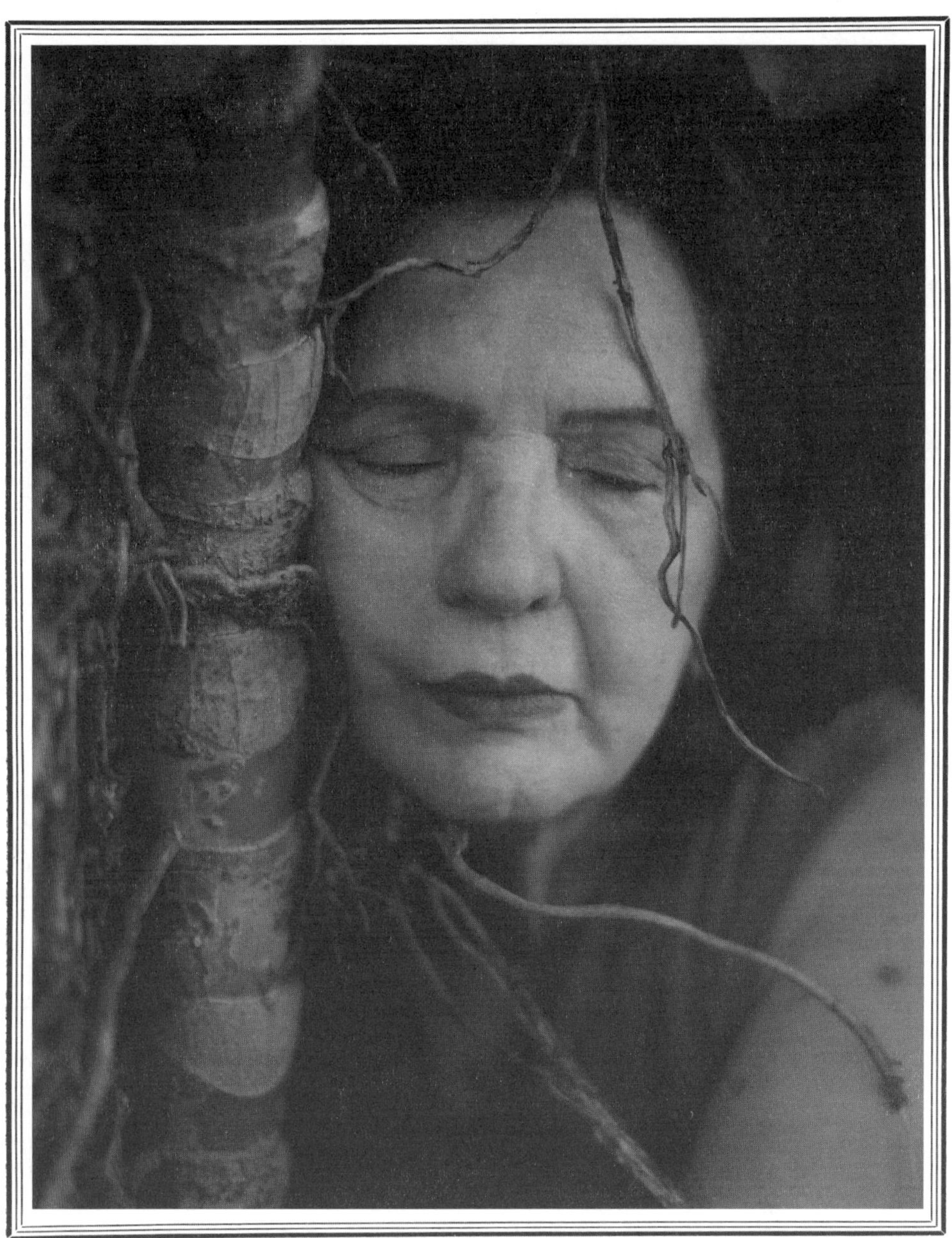

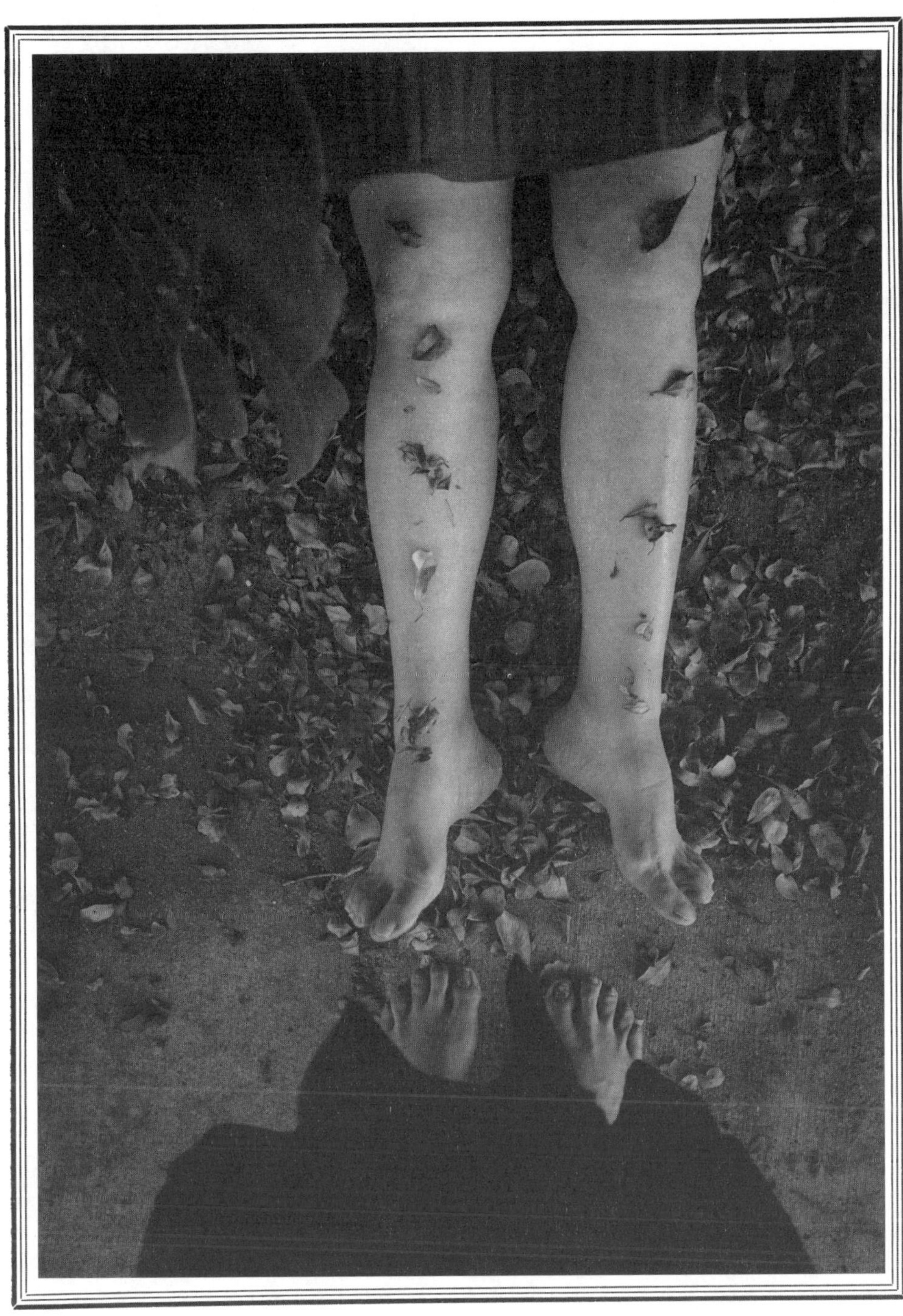

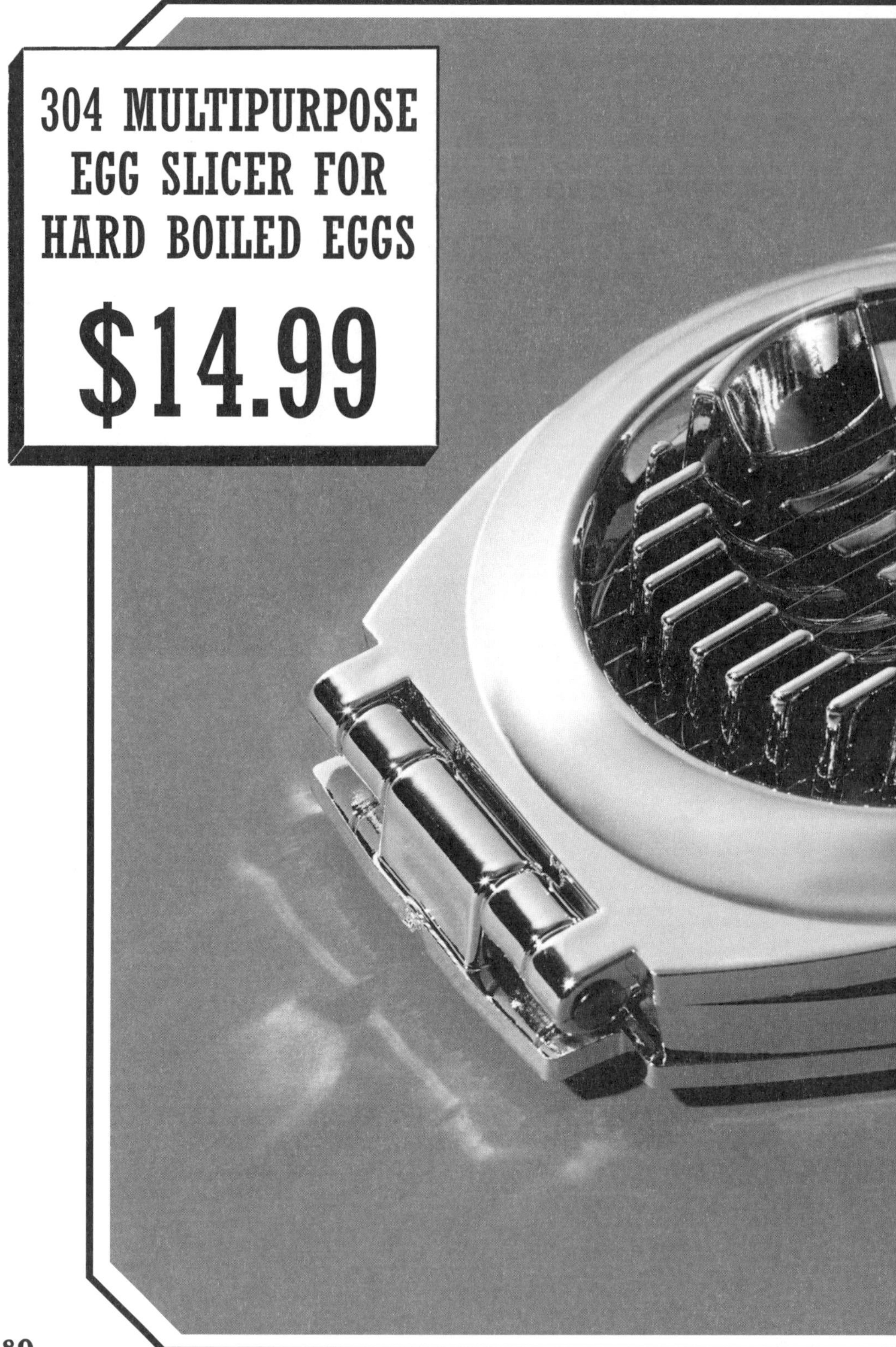
304 MULTIPURPOSE
EGG SLICER FOR
HARD BOILED EGGS
$14.99

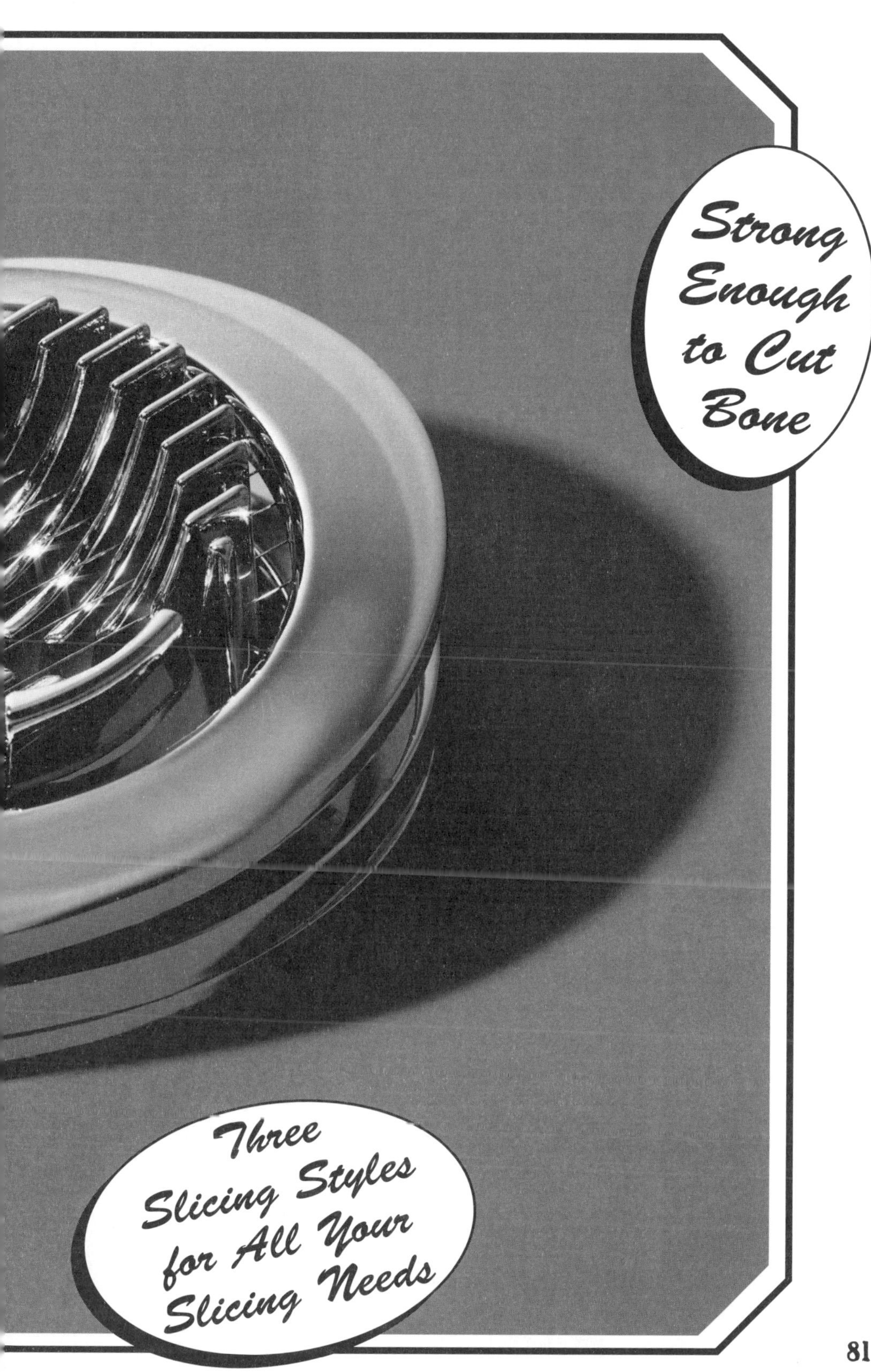
Strong Enough to Cut Bone
Three Slicing Styles for All Your Slicing Needs

retrouver le son
de la mer
les vagues qui apaisent
laisser venir l'écume

accepter
les traces qui s'effacent

mais ne jamais oublier

et enfin pouvoir dire, maman.

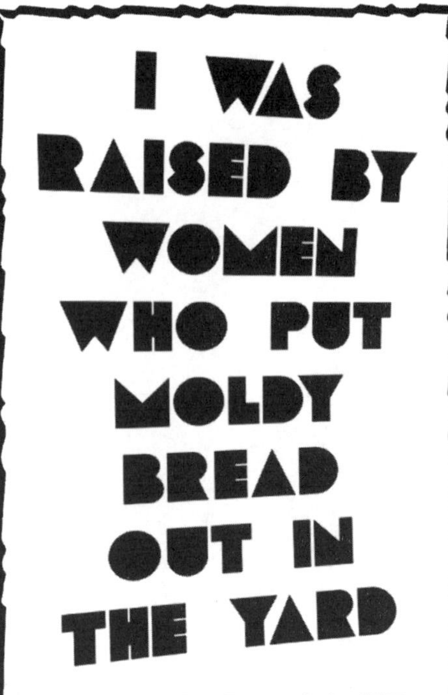

I think, being strained by the situation too. Today we had a new, young lady Pete who hadn't yet received her postal uniform, she was delivering mail in blue jeans with a USPS vest over her t- shirt. Not surprisingly, she mixed up our mail. We got all the mail for the family next door, Natalie's family.

I've had to adopt the neurotic habit of washing my hands every time I check the mail so I didn't notice the mixup until after the scrub down. Luckily, Natalie's whole family was out in the front yard when I went back out with their handful of mail. Her little sister was playing attentively with the yappy white dog, her brother was practicing hitting a baseball into a small backstop net his father has fastened up since the parks have been closed. Her father was there too, critiquing the boy's swing. I thought Natalie's mother was digging weeds when I called over the fence but she stood up with a baggie in one hand and a plastic glove on the other, apparently the chore of picking up after the sister's dog had fallen on the mother. It's been almost three years since Natalie died but I still get tense about talking to her mother. The dogshit glove was just awkward enough to be an ice breaker though. I chuckled a little and said, "sorry, they brought us your mail." I set the envelopes on the fence, she asked about the new baby. Boy or girl? I told her we had a daughter. She took a deep breath, smiled and asked me to hug baby girl for her. I said I would and I did.

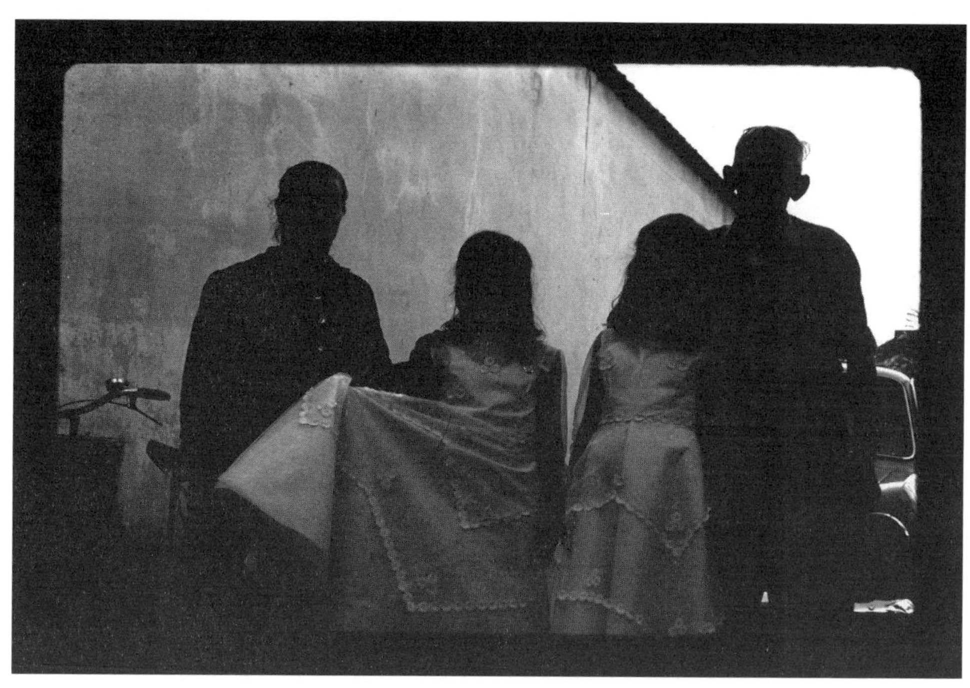

Ithaca College

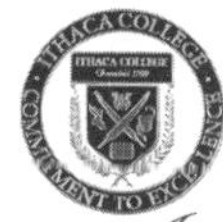

Ithaca New York

The Trustees of Ithaca College,

upon the recommendation of the Faculty have conferred upon

Karine Baptiste

the degree

Master of Fine Arts

with all the honors, rights and privileges appertaining thereto.

In Witness Whereof, *under the seal of the College, the signatures of its duly authorized officers are hereunto affixed August 15, 2020.*

La Jerne Terry Cornish, Ph.D.
Provost and Sr. Vice President Academic Affairs

Shirley M. Collado, Ph.D.
President

INDEX

INDEX

P

Q

R

S

T

U

W

Y

Z

ACKNOWLEDGEMENTS

We would like to thank Nicholas Muellner and Catherine Taylor for their extraordinary vision in creating this MFA program and for their careful guidance with our individual projects. We are grateful for the incredible faculty who shared their knowledge and illuminated new avenues for our work: Stephanie Barber, Lucas Blalock, Tisa Bryant, Bruno Ceschel, Danielle Dutton, Tonya M. Foster, David Hartt, Whitney Hubbs, Jibade-Khalil Huffman, Erica Hunt, Justine Kurland, David Levine, Diana Khoi Nguyen, Mark Nowak, Res, Elana Schlenker, and Paul Soulellis. Also, thank you to our peers: Matt Baczewski, Saxon Baird, Raegan Bird, Andre Bradley, Robert Contreras II, Daax, Hugo Gallo, Nan Heyneman, Shantal Kim, K. Kovacs, Pablo Lerma, Carla Liesching, Jared Lindahl, Melani Elissa Lopez, Martha Ormiston, Nina Perlman, Laura Pierson, John Rufo, Kirslyn Schell-Smith, Hyacinth Schukis, Amy Schuessler, Dale Small, John Smieska, Janet Solval, Kelsey Sucena and the extended Image Text community for sharing work, inspiration, and conversation over these years. And lastly we want to thank Jason Fulford, who brought old catalogs, a record player, a new-old typewriter, a paper cutter and a collaborative spirit to facilitate the creation of this book. Thank you for your care and attentiveness; it's been a joy to work with you.

EVERYTHING MUST GO!

Design by Jason Fulford

Interior printed at Linco Printing
Long Island City, New York

Cover printed at The Arm Letterpress
Brooklyn, New York

First printing, edition of 1000

ISBN: 978-1-7334971-3-8

Available through ARTBOOK/D.A.P.
75 Broad Street, Suite 630 NYC 10004
www.artbook.com

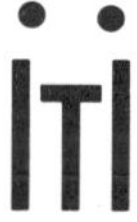

Image Text Ithaca Press

Editors:
Catherine Taylor
Nicholas Muellner

DEAR READER:

We hope you find something in this collection of texts and images to hold; something that makes you think or cry or smile. The featured work was developed both in Ithaca, New York and from our varied homes across the United States and Europe during a time of collective loss and uncertainty. The majority of our years as graduate students in the Image Text MFA Program were spent navigating changes and restrictions due to the Covid-19 pandemic.

Each of our projects reveal distinct vision and purpose, and in this publication we sought to collaborate and play. For you, we've cast fragments, stories, insights, and images. The works bounce against one another and each page conjures a unique image-text experience. We hope you enjoy the distinct pieces and the spaces between.

Cable documents glimpses of life as a father, negotiating inside and outside perspectives. Caiti laments the burden of images and plunges her hands into the dirt. Eleanor contemplates memory, home, and connection; she looks outward from empty rooms into changing weather. Erika offers rituals of healing and thinks about relationships of mothers and mothering. Irit considers family and negotiates the ephemeral space of home movies and visual memory recast in language. Karine asks questions of places, memories and translation; including how language translates on the page. Marissa opens a side door for desire and citrus. Michael reflects on mortality and the potential lives of objects as mediated through technology. Will examines the intersections of geology, time, the body, and climate crisis.

Through this collage of offerings, we hope that you take what you need. After a year of letting go, we extend this book toward new possibilities. Thank you, Reader, for your time. We deeply appreciate you joining us here and hope you return to use this collection as a space of both levity and somber presence. Nothing can stay because *Everything Must Go!*

Yours,

Karine BAPTISTE
Caiti BORRUSO
Eleanor EICHENBAUM
Cable HOOVER
Marissa IAMARTINO
Will MATSUDA
Erika MORILLO
Michael POPP
Irit REINHEIMER